Lower Intermediate

Message
Delivered

Paragraph Writing and Presentation

Leonid Yoffe
Atsushi Chiba
Shoma Aota
Akira Morita

NAN'UN-DO

音声ファイル 無料 DL のご案内

このテキストの音声を無料で視聴（ストリーミング）・ダウンロードできます。自習用音声としてご活用ください。
以下のサイトにアクセスしてテキスト番号で検索してください。

https://nanun-do.com テキスト番号 [**512029**]

※ 無線 LAN（WiFi）に接続してのご利用を推奨いたします。

※ 音声ダウンロードは Zip ファイルでの提供になります。
お使いの機器によっては別途ソフトウェア（アプリケーション）
の導入が必要となります。

Message Delivered <Lower Intermediate> 音声ダウンロードページは
左記の QR コードからもご利用になれます。

はしがき

　本書 *Message Delivered <Lower Intermediate>* は、パラグラフ・ライティング（paragraph writing）をプレゼンテーション（presentation）へとつなげることによって学習者の発信力を強化するレベル別英語教材の基礎編として作成されました。学習者の習熟度に応じて編纂された本シリーズの共通した主な意図と特徴は次の通りです。

1. パラグラフ・ライティングの基礎、つまりその書式（format）、構造（structure）、使うべき表現（expressions）をきちんと身に着ける。
2. それらを的確に使いながら、英語の論理構成（logic）と展開法（organization）にのっとり的確に自分の考えを伝えることができる。
3. しっかりとしたライティングの基本を身に着け、まとめられた自分の考え、意見を同じ論理構成を持ったプレゼンテーションの形として口頭で発表できる。
4. プレゼンテーションの要点を、発表者（presenter）としてプレゼンテーションを行うことによって学ぶだけでなく、より重要な 聴き手（audience）の視点からの反省によって身に着ける。
5. これらに加えて、特に発信にとって重要な文法項目について整理を行う。

　これらは英語のスキル面での学習の要点にもなるわけですが、それが本シリーズの最終的な目標ではありません。最終的な目標は、

a. 論理的な議論の展開（場合によっては日本語のそれとは違った）方法の基礎を知ること
b. その論理の展開法を用いて物事を考え、自分の考えを、説得力を持って効率的に、そして正確に聴き手に伝えられ、同時にそうできるという自信を得ること
c. 根拠を持った発言により、それを聞く人々から信頼を得、グローバル人材の備えるべき発信面での能力向上を図ること

　というものです。こうした目標を、本シリーズは学習者の習熟度に合わせたレベル別の構成によって、無理なく達成できるように企画されました。

　その中で、本書 *Message Delivered <Lower Intermediate>* は、特にそれぞれの基礎、基本となる最も重要な点を精査してタスクに盛り込んでいます。この基礎は、もちろん本シリーズの他の教科書にも共通するものですし、またこの基礎を理解できれば、その後の発展は比較的容易なものであるはずです。そうした発展は、学習者の皆さんが、何度も練習し、実際に書き、発表することで体験しながら行ってください。それが著者一同の望みです。

　なお、刊行にあたっては、株式会社南雲堂の加藤敦さんに企画面を含め多くの助言をいただきました。加藤さんの忍耐力なくしては、本シリーズの完成はなかったでしょう。また、中原緑さんには、内容の点検も含め最終的な編集場面でご面倒をお掛けしました。この場を借りて御礼申し上げます。

著者一同
2019 年盛夏

本書の使い方

　本書 *Message Delivered <Lower Intermediate>* は、皆さんに次のような技能を身につけて欲しいという思いで編集されています。

1. パラグラフ・ライティング（paragraph writing）の基礎を学び、簡単なパラグラフ（paragraph）を書くことができる。
2. 読み手（reader）や聞き手（audience）を意識したパラグラフを書くことができる。
3. そのパラグラフを基にプレゼンテーション（presentation）原稿を作成し、効果的な口頭発表ができる。

　この目標を達成するために、本書を以下の Part I 〜 Part III で構成しました。

Part I（Unit 1-4）　　　パラグラフの書式（format）と基本構造（structure）を学びます。
Part II（Unit 5-10）　　パラグラフの型ごとに、論理構成（logic）や展開法（organization）を学びます。
Part III（Unit 11-14）　プレゼンテーションの基本構造と効果的な発表の仕方について学びます。

● Part I

　Part I ではパラグラフの基本構造をまとめて学習します。説明文を読んで、練習問題を解答していきましょう。自然にパラグラフの構造が理解できるはずです。ここで学習したことが Part II 以降で行うパラグラフ作成の基本になります。パラグラフの構造が分からなくなったら、ここに戻って理解を確かめましょう。

● Part II

　Part II では Unit ごとに 1 つずつパラグラフの型を取り上げます。各 Unit にはトピックが設定されており、型を意識しながらトピックに関するパラグラフを仕上げていきます。Part II はいくつかのセクションに分かれています。

Warm Up

　各 Unit のトピックに関するアンケートに答えます。問題や選択肢は Unit 後半でパラグラフを作成する際のヒントにもなっています。しっかりと考えて回答しましょう。

Paragraph Analysis

　各 Unit で扱うパラグラフの型について学びます。その型の展開の仕方や特徴を学んだ後、練習問題でパラグラフを分析して、構造を理解しましょう。ここで、論理構成や展開の仕方をしっかりと身につけることで、この後のアウトラインやパラグラフの作成に無理なく移っていくことができます。

| Grammar for Writing

　英文を書くときに注意しておきたい文法項目をまとめました。練習問題を通して、時制の使い分けや助動詞の意味、接続詞（等位接続詞と従属接続詞）、形容詞と副詞などの基本的な項目を再確認します。このセクションだけで詳細に文法を説明することはできませんので、分からない文法事項が出てきたら、参考書や辞書などで調べるようにしましょう。

| Vocabulary for the Topic

　トピックに関連する語句の意味を練習問題を通して確認するセクションです。分からない語句についてはあらかじめ辞書などで調べておきましょう。アウトラインを作成する際のヒントにもなっているので、ここで学ぶ語句をきっかけに考えをまとめることも可能です。

| Outline

　パラグラフを実際に書くための準備段階です。指示に従って、主題文、支持文、まとめの文に書くことを整理しておきます。日本語での整理、語句レベルでの整理、文レベルでの整理、と書き方はいくつか考えられますが、どの方法で整理するかは授業での指示に従ってください。

| Writing

　Outline で整理した内容をパラグラフの形に整えていく課題です。全体の構造を意識しながら、基本に忠実なパラグラフを書くようにしましょう。

● Part III

　Part III では、プレゼンテーションの基本構造を学びながら、Unit 10 で書いたパラグラフをプレゼンテーション用の原稿に書き換えていきます。Part を通して、説明文を読みながら練習問題を進めていくことで、1 つのプレゼンテーション原稿が完成する仕組みになっています。各 Unit には視覚資料の作り方に関するセクションも付いています。効果的なプレゼンテーションを構成する一部として挑戦してみてください。

　また、Part の最後には実際にプレゼンテーションを行い評価する Unit があります。聴衆に聞いてもらうように話す練習と、人の発表を注意深く聞く練習を行い、相互に評価することを経験します。

Contents

UNIT 1 パラグラフの構造

書式（**Formatting**）

　効率よく情報を伝達するには、決められた書式（formatting）に沿って文章を作成しなければなりません。学術的な文章を雑誌などに投稿する場合でも、それぞれの投稿先によって書式が決められています。本書では、以下の書式に沿ってパラグラフの作成を行います。なお、以下の書式は、ワープロソフトで文章を作成することを前提にしていますが、手書きの場合もこれに準じて作成しましょう。

タイトル（**title**）：最初の行にタイトルを書く。パラグラフの内容が想像できるようなものが好ましいが、あまり長くならないようにする。
　中央揃えにして、すべての単語の最初の文字を大文字にする。ただし、冠詞、前置詞、接続詞、代名詞などは、タイトルの先頭以外では原則的に小文字にする。

名前と日付（**name and date**）：ヘッダーに右寄せで名前と提出日を記入する。

インデント（**indentation**）：最初の文は3〜5文字程度、右側に字下げをする。

行間（**line space**）：十分な行間を取る。目安は1行おきの行間。ワープロソフトの場合、行数を25行程度に設定する。

余白（**margin**）：上下左右に十分な余白を設定する。目安は、およそ以下の通り。
　上 35mm
　下 30mm
　左右 30mm

配置（**alignment**）：「両端揃え」もしくは「左揃え」にする。

フォント（**font**）：Century や Times New Roman が一般的。本文の文字サイズは12ポイント程度の見やすいサイズにする。タイトルは本文よりも少し大きなサイズにする。

改行（**line break**）：語の途中での改行はできるだけ避ける。また、1文ごとに改行するようなことはしない。

用紙（**paper**）：A4用紙

Takashi Yamamoto
April 13, 20XX

How Birds Fly

　Birds fly mainly in three ways. One way is to fly by flapping their wings. Up-and-down motion of their wings pushes them forward. Another way is to fly by gliding without flapping their wings. They keep their wings stretched out to go up. The third way is to fly by soaring in a rising air current. This is a special kind of gliding, so birds do not flap their wings. In short, birds can fly by flapping their wings, gliding, or soaring in the sky.

次のパラグラフについて、書式上の問題点を指摘しましょう。

Takashi Yamamoto
April 13, 20XX

How birds fly
Birds fly mainly in three ways.
One way is to fly by flapping their wings.
Up-and-down motion of their wings pushes them forward.
Another way is to fly by gliding without flapping their wings.
They keep their wings stretched out to go up.
The third way is to fly by soaring in a rising air current.
This is a special kind of gliding, so birds do not flap their wings.
In short, birds can fly by flapping their wings, gliding, or soaring in the sky.

Paragraph Structure

一つの話題について述べているいくつかの文のかたまりのことをパラグラフ（paragraph）と言います。パラグラフは、以下の構成要素を順序良く並べることによって読者に伝わりやすいものになります。

主題文（**Topic Sentence**）：パラグラフのトピックとそのトピックに対する筆者の考えを提示する文。通常パラグラフの先頭に置かれる。

支持文（**Supporting Sentences**）：主題文で提示した考えを裏付けるために、具体例や理由を述べたり、より踏み込んだ情報を示したりする文。具体例や理由などの数に応じて、複数の支持文を置くことになる。

ディテール（**Details**）：支持文に続いて、支持文を詳しく説明する文。それぞれの支持文に1〜2文加えるのが普通。

まとめの文（**Concluding Sentence**）：パラグラフの内容をまとめたり、主題文の主張を別のことばで言い換えたりしてパラグラフ全体をまとめる文。パラグラフの最後に置かれる。

＊ 本書では、主題文（1文）＋支持文（3文）＋ディテール（3文）＋まとめの文（1文）の8文からなるパラグラフを書く練習をしていきます。

Takashi Yamamoto
April 13, 20XX

How birds fly

Birds fly mainly in three ways. One way is to fly by
`Topic Sentence`　　　　　　　`Supporting Sentence 1`
flapping their wings. Up-and-down motion of their wings
`Detail`
pushes them forward. Another way is to fly by gliding
`Supporting Sentence 2`
without flapping their wings. They keep their wings
`Detail`
stretched out to go up. The third way is to fly by soaring
`Supporting Sentence 3`
in a rising air current. This is a special kind of gliding,
`Detail`
so birds do not flap their wings. In short, birds can fly
`Concluding Sentence`
by flapping their wings, gliding, or soaring in the sky.

3つの支持文を、文頭の主題文、文末のまとめの文で挟み込むような形にする。

3つの支持文には、それぞれ1つのディテールを付ける。

合計8つの文で一つのパラグラフを完成させる。

次のパラグラフを読んで、後の問に答えましょう。

Why My Hometown is a Great Place for Families

(1) My hometown is a good place to raise children. (2) First, there is a large park in the town center. (3) It's a wonderful place for families to mingle and for children to play together. (4) Second, there are a few libraries with children's books. (5) They sometimes hold special story-telling events which kids really enjoy. (6) Lastly, there is a large children's hospital. (7) It has some of the best doctors and medical equipment in the country. (8) In short, my town offers very convenient facilities for families with small children.

---

1. 主題文を番号で指摘し、その内容を日本語で説明しましょう。

   主題文（　　　）　　　内容：..

2. 支持文とそれぞれの支持文に続くディテールを番号で指摘し、その内容を日本語で説明しましょう。

   支持文1（　　　）　　　内容：..

   ディテール（　　　）内容：..

   支持文2（　　　）　　　内容：..

   ディテール（　　　）内容：..

   支持文3（　　　）　　　内容：..

   ディテール（　　　）内容：..

3. まとめの文を番号で指摘し、どのようなまとめ方をしているのかを日本語で説明しましょう。

   まとめの文（　　　）　　まとめ方：..

Exercise C

次のパラグラフの空欄に入る文を下から選び、パラグラフを完成しましょう。

English as a Global Language

English-speaking countries can be divided into three groups according to how English is used there. The first group consists of countries in which English is the first language. It includes America, Canada, the UK, and several other countries. (1)_____ (2)_____ _____ The third group comprises countries in which English is studied as a main foreign language. (3)_____ (4)_____ _____

(a) Most of the remaining countries around the world are included in this group.

(b) The second group consists of nations in which English is used as the second or official language.

(c) As you can see, English is truly a global language today.

(d) India, the Philippines, Singapore, and over 50 other nations belong to this group.

Grammar for Writing

文の構造

文の構造の**3**タイプ
英語の文には**3**つのタイプがあります。

1. 単文：S + V の関係が **1** つだけで、主節のみで成り立っている文
   I like coffee.
   Mary did not go to the party.

2. 重文：**2** つ以上の節が等位接続詞で結ばれた文
   I like coffee, and Mary likes tea.
   Mary went to work, but I didn't.

3. 複文：主節の他に従属節を含む文
   We missed our plane because we were stuck in traffic.
   Do you know the man who is talking to Mary?

次のそれぞれの文の誤りを訂正しましょう。

1. Took a walk early in the morning.

2. My brother and I went to the mall last night. But didn't buy anything.

3. My tooth hurt. So I went to the dentist.

4. Tom went to bed, he was tired.

5. although Ken was sick he decided to go out with his out-of-town friends.

Exercise E

与えられた単語を並べ替えて、日本語を英語にしましょう。

1. 私は週に3回ジムに行きます。
   (a / I / go / gym / the / three / times / to / week).

2. 私たちはホッケーの試合を見た後、家に帰りました。
   (a / after / game / hockey / home / we / we / watched / went).

3. 雨が降ったので、道路が濡れています。
   (because / is / it / rained / street / the / wet).

4. 私は年だが、あなたはまだ若い。
   (are / am / but / I / old / you / young).

5. 私が着いたとき、ケイトは誰かと話をしていました。
   (arrived / I / Kate / someone / talking / to / was / when).

UNIT 2 主題文（Topic Sentence）

What is a topic sentence?

● 主題文には次のような特徴や役割があります。

> 主題文の特徴・役割
> 1）パラグラフの先頭に置かれる
> 2）筆者がそのパラグラフで伝えたいこと（主旨：main idea）を 1 文で示す
> 3）読み手に、パラグラフに何が書いてあるのかを予測させる

● 主題文は以下のような基本構造を取ります。

> 主題文の基本構造
> トピック（topic）＋主張（assertion）＋制限 / 条件（limitation / condition）
> 　　S　　　　　　V　　　　　　　　（M）

【例】 Sendai　is an ideal place　to raise children.
　　　トピック　　　主張　　　　　　制限

トピック（**topic**）：パラグラフで取り上げ、論じる話題のことです。パラグラフ全体は 1 トピックで統一されるので、ここで示されるトピックがパラグラフ全体のトピックになります。なお、トピックは必ずしも主語（S）の位置に現れるとは限りませんが、本書では「主題文の主語＝トピック」という形を取ることにします。

主張（**assertion**）：書き手がトピックについて、自分の考えを述べたりコメントしたりする部分です。トッピックについてどのように考えているのかを明確に示すことによって、パラグラフ全体の方向性を決定づけます。

制限 / 条件（**limitation / condition**）：この部分は付けたり付けなかったりしますが、「主張」の範囲を絞り込むことと、主題文以降のパラグラフの展開を明らかにする役割を担います。

次の各文に入る「トピック」を下から選び、主題文を完成しましょう。

1. _____ attracts many tourists because it has several World Heritage sites.

2. _____ contributes to good mental health.

3. _____ can be divided into three groups based on how they fly.

4. _____ are provided for men and women in Japan.

> Flying animals
> Having a pet
> Equal education opportunities
> Nepal

次の各文に入る「主張」を下から選び、主題文を完成しましょう。

1. The smartphone _____ for elderly people.

2. Soccer _____ in Japan.

3. Being a good teacher _____

4. Education _____ in lowering poverty rates.

> plays an important role
> is one of the most popular sports
> is a convenient device
> requires a flexible personality and a lot of patience

Exercise C

次の各文に入る「制限または条件」を下から選び、主題文を完成しましょう。

1. Padel is similar to tennis ....

2. Ichiro Suzuki was one of the best athletes ....

3. Mother's Day is celebrated differently ....

4. El Niño has a strong impact ....

> depending on the country
> playing baseball both in Japan and the US
> on the global climate
> in terms of rules

Exercise D

次のトピックに続く「主張」や「制限または条件」を補って、主題文を完成しましょう。

1. Canada ....

....

2. Hybrid cars ....

....

3. Halloween ....

....

4. Being a good politician ....

....

5. The consumption tax rate ....

Tips for a good topic sentence

適切な主題文を作るために、注意しなければいけないことがあります。

1. あいまいな内容にしない：漠然とした主題文にすると、1パラグラフでは説明しきれなくなってしまいます。制限または条件を加えることで、内容を絞ることができます。
   - × Yoga is good.
   - ○ Yoga is a good workout for mental health.

2. 複数のトピックを盛り込まない：1パラグラフは1トピックで統一されるので、主題文に書くトピックも1つだけになります。
   - × Japanese gardens and Japanese animation are popular all over the world.
   - ○ Japanese gardens are well known around the world.
   - ○ Japanese animation is popular all over the world.

3. 疑問文にしない：読み手に何かを問いかけただけでは、主旨（main idea）を表明することはできません。
   - × What has caused global warming?
   - ○ Global warming has been caused by some human activities.

4. これから書くことの「予告文」にしない：「〜について書きます」と予告しただけでは、主旨（main idea）を表明したことにはなりません。
   - × I am going to write about jaguars, animals facing extinction.
   - ○ Jaguars are in danger of extinction for a number of reasons.

Exercise E

次のそれぞれの文が主題文としてふさわしくない理由を説明しましょう。

1. Does cooking require a lot of skill?

   理由：_____

2. Cellphones and lack of sleep have a negative effect on children's growth.

   理由：_____

3. Hockey is a great sport.

   理由：_____

4. I am going to explain why graduating from college is so important.

   理由：_____

Exercise F

Exercise E のそれぞれの文が主題文としてふさわしい文になるように書き換えましょう。

1. _____

2. _____

3. _____

4. _____

Grammar for Writing

現在形

現在形は常に起こる出来事や状況を表し、次のような場面を表します。

1. 現在の状態（状態動詞が使われる）
   I know Kate's husband.
   Ken lives in Kobe.

2. 現在の習慣的・反復的動作
   Sam plays tennis after school every day.
   Abby walks to school.

3. 一般的真理や事実
   The moon revolves around the earth.
   Water freezes at zero degrees Celsius.

次のそれぞれの文の誤りを訂正しましょう。

1. I'm always eating rice for breakfast.

2. Water made up 65 percent of the human body.

3. Victor is belonging to the soccer club.

4. She practice piano every morning for three hours.

5. All insects are having six legs.

与えられた単語を並べ替えて、日本語を英語にしましょう。

1. クリスは毎朝髪を洗います。
   (Chris / every / hair / his / morning / washes).

2. クジラは哺乳類に分類されます。
   (are / as / classified / mammals / whales).

3. 私は商社に勤めています。
   (a / company / for / I / trading / work).

4. この写真の男性は私の伯父にとても似ています。
   (closely / in / man / my / picture / resembles / the / this / uncle).

5. 私の父は、夜はたいていテレビを見ています。
   (evening / dad / in / my / television / the / usually / watches).

UNIT 3　支持文 (Supporting Sentences)

What are supporting sentences?

● 支持文には次のような特徴や役割があります。

> 支持文の特徴・役割
> 1) 主題文とまとめの文の間に置かれる
> 2) 主題文で提示した考えを裏付ける（サポートする）
> 3) 裏付けのために、理由や具体例、根拠などを提示して説明する
> 4) 支持文の展開の仕方によって、パラグラフを「列挙のパラグラフ」「時系列のパラグラフ」「比較のパラグラフ」のような目的に合わせた型に分類することができる

● 主題文と支持文は以下のような関係になっています。

【主題文】
Birds fly mainly in three ways.

 サポート　　 サポート　　 サポート

【支持文 1】
One way is to fly by flapping their wings.

【支持文 2】
Another way is to fly by gliding without flapping their wings.

【支持文 3】
The third way is to fly by soaring in a rising air current.

次の主題文にふさわしい支持文を 3 つ選び、下の①〜③に記入しましょう。

主題文：

A *furoshiki*, or a Japanese wrapping cloth, has been popular even among non-Japanese people for a number of reasons.

【支持文】
・It is very ecological.
・It is out of date.
・It is versatile.
・It is very beautiful.

① ....

② ....

③ ....

What are the details?

● ディテールには次のような特徴や役割があります。

ディテールの特徴・役割
1) 支持文に続いて、支持文を詳しく説明する
2) 支持文を噛み砕いた説明がなされたり、支持文の妥当性を示すために「事実」「例」「引用」「統計データ」などが提示されたりする
3) 各支持文に 1 〜 2 文付けられるのが普通だが、無い場合もある
（＊本書では、1 つの支持文に 1 つのディテールを付けるようにします）

● 支持文とディテールは以下のような関係になっています。

┌─────────────────────┐   ┌─────────────────────┐   ┌─────────────────────┐
│ 【支持文 1】   │   │ 【支持文 2】   │   │ 【支持文 3】   │
│ One way is to fly by │   │ Another way is to fly│   │ The third way is to │
│ flapping their wings.│   │ by gliding without   │   │ fly by soaring in a │
│   │   │ flapping their wings.│   │ rising air current. │
└─────────────────────┘   └─────────────────────┘   └─────────────────────┘

 説明   説明   説明

┌─────────────────────┐   ┌─────────────────────┐   ┌─────────────────────┐
│ 【ディテール 1】   │   │ 【ディテール 2】   │   │ 【ディテール 3】   │
│ Up-and-down motion   │   │ They keep their   │   │ This is a special kind│
│ of their wings pushes│   │ wings stretched out │   │ of gliding, so birds do│
│ them forward.   │   │ to go up.   │   │ not flap their wings. │
└─────────────────────┘   └─────────────────────┘   └─────────────────────┘

Exercise B

Exercise A で選んだ①〜③のそれぞれの支持文にふさわしいディテールを選び、下の❶〜❸に記入しましょう。

┌───┐
│ 【details】   │
│ ・It comes in many colors and designs.   │
│ ・Even elderly people rarely use it.   │
│ ・You can use it over and over instead of throwing it away.   │
│ ・Since it can be wrapped around items of different shapes, you can carry your clothes or │
│   a large sake bottle in it.   │
└───┘

❶ ....

❷ ....

❸ ....

How to write a cohesive paragraphs

● どの文が支持文なのかを明確にすることで、パラグラフを読みやすいものにすることができます。

● たとえば **3** つの理由を支持文で挙げる場合、
The first reason is ...　The second reason is ...　The final reason is ...
といった表現を使えば、読み手は支持文を探す必要もなく負担なく読むことができます。

● 支持文を明確にするために使われる表現はパラグラフの型によって多少違いますが、最もよく使われるのは次の表現です。
First (Firstly), ...　Second (Secondly), ...　Third (Thirdly / Finally), ...

Exercise C

次の文章の（　　）内に適切な語を入れましょう。

　A *furoshiki*, or a Japanese wrapping cloth, has been popular even among non-Japanese for a number of reasons. The (① 　　　　　　　　) reason is that it is very ecological. You can use it over and over instead of throwing it away. (② 　　　　　), it is versatile. Since it can be wrapped around items of different shapes, you can carry your clothes or a large sake bottle in it. (③ 　　　　　), it is very beautiful. It comes in many colors and designs.

Exercise D

STEP に従って、パラグラフを作成しましょう。

STEP 1

次の主題文にふさわしい支持文を 3 つ書きましょう。

主題文： *Tenugui*, or a Japanese hand towel, is a popular souvenir from Japan for several reasons.

① _____

② _____

③ _____

STEP 2

STEP 1 の①〜③の各支持文にふさわしいディテールを書きましょう。

❶ _____

❷ _____

❸ _____

STEP 3

STEP 1, 2 の主題文、支持文、ディテールをまとめて、まとまりのある文章にしましょう。

_____

_____

_____

_____

_____

Grammar for Writing

過去形

過去形は過去のあるときに起こったことを表し、次のような場面を表します。

1. 過去の状態
   I really thought that she was a responsible person.
   Alice belonged to the brass band club at high school.

2. 過去の習慣的・反復的動作
   I always went to bed late during the summer break.
   My sister helped me with my homework when I was a small child.

3. 過去の一度きりの動作
   I met my husband in 2001.
   Tom bought a new laptop three days ago.

次のそれぞれの文の誤りを訂正しましょう。

1. I was loving reading when I was a child.

2. Derek studies for three hours every day when he was a high school student.

3. I getted a speeding ticket yesterday.

4. Patsy was remembering her aunt's birthday.

5. Are you hearing what the guide just said?

与えられた単語を並べ替えて、日本語を英語にしましょう。

1. 私は今朝リタと電話で話をしました。
   (I / morning / on / phone / Rita / talked / the / this / with).

2. あのパン屋さんはいつもいいにおいがしていました。
   (always / bakery / good / smelled / the).

3. 私はよく博物館で時間を過ごしました。
   (I / in / museums / often / spent / time).

4. 事故はその店の前で起こりました。
   (accident / front / in / happened / of / store / the / the).

5. 多くの年配者がまだ幽霊を信じていると聞きました。
   (heard / believed / ghosts / I / in / many / people / senior / still / that).

UNIT 4　まとめの文（Concluding Sentence）

What is a concluding sentence?

● まとめの文には次のような特徴や役割があります。

> **まとめの文の特徴・役割**
>
> 1）パラグラフの最後に置かれる
> 2）パラグラフが終了することを示す
> 3）読み手に、筆者の考えやそれに対する裏付けのポイントを再確認させる

● まとめの文の冒頭にはパラグラフの終了を示す表現が使われます。

> **パラグラフの終了を示す表現**
>
> In conclusion, ...　　In summary, ...　　To sum up, ...　　To conclude, ...
> To summarize, ...　　In short, ...

● まとめの文には 2 種類の書き方があります。

> **まとめの文の書き方**
>
> 1）主題文を別の言葉や表現で言い換える
> 2）パラグラフのポイント（支持文のポイント）をまとめる

【例】

1）主題文の言い換え

　　主題文：　Nepal attracts many tourists because it has several outstanding World Heritage sites.

　　まとめの文：　In short, these sites have made Nepal a popular tourist destination.

2) パラグラフのポイントのまとめ

主題文： Birds fly mainly in three ways.

支持文：
1) One way is to fly by flapping their wings.
2) Another way is to fly by gliding without flapping their wings.
3) The third way is to fly by soaring in a rising air current.

⬇

まとめの文： In short, birds can fly by flapping their wings, gliding, or soaring in the sky.

Exercise A

次のそれぞれの主題文を別の言葉や表現で言い換えて、まとめの文を作りましょう。

1. 主題文： The smartphone is a convenient device for elderly people.

   まとめの文： ....

2. 主題文： Soccer is one of the most popular sports in Japan.

   まとめの文： ....

3. 主題文： Having a pet can have a positive effect on mental health.

   まとめの文： ....

4. 主題文： Education plays an important role in lowering poverty rates.

   まとめの文： ....

Exercise B

次の主題文と３つの支持文を読んで、パラグラフのポイントをまとめた「まとめの文」を作りましょう。

1. 主題文： Latte is different from café au lait in several ways.

   支持文：
   1) Latte is made with espresso, while café au lait usually uses filtered coffee.
   2) Latte uses steamed milk and milk foam, although café au lait is made with heated milk only.
   3) Latte contains much more milk than café au lait.

   まとめの文： ....

   ....

2. 主題文： The Japan national soccer team has become stronger as it went through some key historic events.

支持文： 1) The professional soccer league, called J. league, started with ten clubs in 1993.
2) The national team narrowly missed the ticket to the World Cup in 1994.
3) Japan co-hosted the 2002 World Cup with South Korea.

まとめの文： _____

_____

Exercise C

次の文章の下線部にまとめの文を書いて、パラグラフを完成しましょう。

A *furoshiki*, or a Japanese wrapping cloth, has been popular even among non-Japanese people for a number of reasons. The first reason is that it is very ecological. You can use it over and over instead of throwing it away. Secondly, it is versatile. Since it can be wrapped around items of different shapes, you can carry your clothes or a large sake bottle in it. Lastly, it is very beautiful. It comes in many colors and designs. _____

_____

_____

Exercise D

Unit 3 の Exercise D（p.24）で作成した文章にまとめの文を付けて、パラグラフを完成しましょう。

_____

_____

_____

_____

_____

_____

What is a good title?

● 良いタイトルには次のような特徴があります。

> 良いタイトルの特徴
> 1) 読み手の興味をそそる
> 2) パラグラフの内容を想像することができる
> 3) あまり長くない（文にはしない）

● タイトルは、パラグラフを書く前に決めても、書き終わった後に決めても構いません。それぞれ次のような手法を取ることがあります。

　1) パラグラフを書く前に決める場合：パラグラフの主旨（main idea）から思いつくキーワードを使って、タイトルに主旨を織り込むようにする

　2) 一通り書き終わった後に決める場合：パラグラフで使った重要な語句を選び、タイトルに組み込むようにする

Exercise E

Exercise C と Exercise D で作成したパラグラフにタイトルを付けましょう。

Exercise C のパラグラフのタイトル

_____

Exercise D のパラグラフのタイトル

_____

Grammar for Writing

Part I

現在完了形

　現在完了形は過去の出来事が現在と何らかの関係を持っていることを表します。過去の出来事が現在とどのように関係するかよって、3つの用法に分けられます。

1. 継続：過去に始まったことが現在も続いている

   I have been in New York since last month.

   Kathy has wanted to become a dancer.

2. 経験：現在までに何かを経験している

   I have seen the movie three times.

   Have you ever been to Italy?

3. 完了・結果：現在までに動作が完了していたり、過去の出来事が現在に何らかの結果を招いていたりする

   Ken has just gone to school.

   I have lost my passport.

Exercise F

次のそれぞれの文の誤りを訂正しましょう。

1. Mr. Takeda have written five books about EU economy.

   _____

2. Have you took a bath yet?

   _____

3. Susan has taught college geography 10 years ago.

   _____

4. We has just arrived at the restaurant.

   _____

5. I have known Ken since three months.

   _____

Exercise G

与えられた単語を並べ替えて、日本語を英語にしましょう。

1. 学生たちはまだ課題を終えていない。
   (assignments / finished / haven't / students / their / yet).

   _____

2. 私は6年間中国で働いている。
   (China / for / have / I / in / six / worked / years).

   _____

3. マリアは大切な書類を無くしてしまった。
   (an / document / has / important / lost / Maria).

   _____

4. ロバートと話したことがありますか？
   (ever / have / Robert / talked / you / to)?

   _____

5. 私たちは今学期が始まってから、2回のテストを受けている。
   (already / had / have / semester / since / started / tests / this / two / we).

   _____

IoT製品の機能を説明しよう（Listing）

インターネットに接続される端末といえば、パソコンやタブレット、スマートフォンなどが考えられますが、最近ではエアコンや冷蔵庫などインターネットに接続可能な家電も出始めてきています。このように身の回りのあらゆるものがインターネットにつながる仕組みのことを IoT (Internet of Things：モノのインターネット) といいます。IoT は私たちの生活をどのように変えていくのでしょうか。

Part II

Warm Up

A. 次のアンケートに答えましょう。

1. How many smart appliances do you have at home?

　　☐ one　　　　　　　　　　☐ two
　　☐ three　　　　　　　　　☐ other (　　　　　　　　　　)

2. Which of the following do you think should become smart devices?

　　☐ vending machines　　　☐ traffic lights
　　☐ mailboxes　　　　　　　☐ garbage cans

3. Which function(s) do you think smart home appliances should have?

　　☐ pet monitoring function　☐ remote control
　　☐ voice-guided navigation　☐ other (　　　　　　　　　　)

4. What should IoT technology be used for?

　　☐ for healthcare　　　　　☐ for crime prevention
　　☐ for amusement　　　　　☐ other (　　　　　　　　　　)

5. Who will benefit from IoT technology the most?

　　☐ young people　　　　　　☐ elderly people
　　☐ business people　　　　　☐ other (　　　　　　　　　　)

B. アンケートを基に、ペアで会話をしてみましょう。

Paragraph Analysis

列挙のパラグラフ

　主題文の主張を裏付ける項目を、支持文に逐一挙げていく展開方法です。ディテールではそれぞれの項目について少し詳しく説明します。列挙のパラグラフを作る際は、それぞれ独立した項目を挙げることが重要です。似通ったものになってしまうと、読者が混乱してしまいます。

列挙のパラグラフで用いられる表現

First (Firstly), ...　　　　　　Second (Secondly), ...

Third (Thirdly / Finally), ...　One reason is ...

Another (A second) reason is ...　A third (final) reason is ...

Model Paragraph

Smart Vending Machines

　　Smart vending machines offer convenient features for the public. First of all, the stock is monitored electronically. As a result, you rarely see "sold-out" messages on the machine. Secondly, the machine allows you to pay with a credit card or use e-money. You do not have to worry about carrying enough cash. Finally, the temperature inside the machine is automatically adjusted. Thus, your drink or sandwich will be just the right temperature. In short, vending machines have become very sophisticated and offer really helpful features to consumers.

Exercise A

日本語で空欄を埋めて、モデル・パラグラフの構造を確認しましょう。

主題文の内容

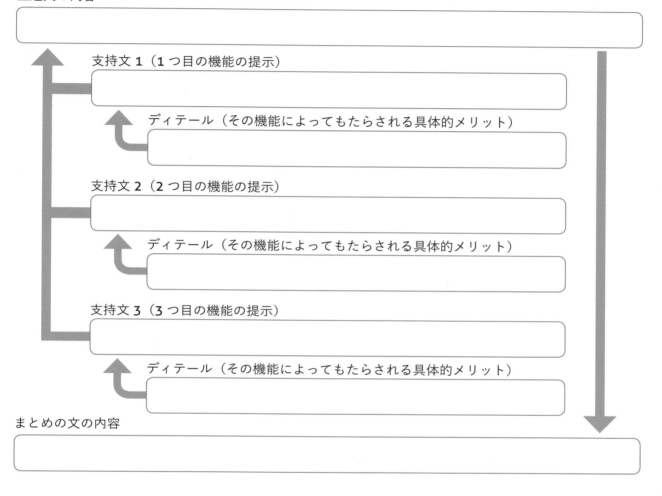

支持文 1（1 つ目の機能の提示）

ディテール（その機能によってもたらされる具体的メリット）

支持文 2（2 つ目の機能の提示）

ディテール（その機能によってもたらされる具体的メリット）

支持文 3（3 つ目の機能の提示）

ディテール（その機能によってもたらされる具体的メリット）

まとめの文の内容

Exercise B

（　　　）内に適切な語を入れて、パラグラフを完成しましょう。

Future Smart Garbage Cans

Future garbage cans for public use will offer three advantages for our community. (① 　　　　　), they can reduce the cost of garbage collection. Thanks to a sensor inside a can, waste management services can collect garbage efficiently. (② 　　　　　), smart cans can help keep towns clean. Garbage will be collected before it overflows. (③ 　　　　　), such garbage cans can contribute to keeping streets safe. If someone tries to put a dangerous object into a garbage can, a sensor will detect it and alert the police. To sum up, the new technology will make waste management less costly while keeping our communities cleaner and safer.

Grammar for Writing

現在進行形

現在進行形は現在進行中の動作を表し、次のような用法があります。

1. まさに今進行中の動作
   Ken is taking a shower now.
   I am writing an e-mail to my friend.

2. 現在を含む一定期間中に進行中の動作
   Our college is building a new campus.
   I am taking ten courses this semester.

3. 一時的な状態
   I am thinking about my test tomorrow.
   Ted is having a good time.

Exercise C

日本語の意味に合うように、与えられた動詞を適切な形に直しましょう。

1. Tom _____ a video game on his phone.　(play)

   トムはスマートフォンでゲームをしています。

2. Mike _____ a fitness tracker.　(have)

   マイクは活動量計を持っています。

3. _____ you _____ your e-mail now?　(check)

   今、eメールをチェックしているのですか？

4. I _____ the web.　(surf)

   私はネットサーフィンをしています。

5. My friends came over, and we _____ our favorite movies now.　(stream)

   友だちがやって来て、今お気に入りの映画を見ています。

Exercise D

与えられた単語を並べ替えて、日本語を英語にしましょう。

1. その掃除機にはセンサーが付いています。
   (a / cleaner / has / sensor / the / vacuum).

2. 今、マックに新しいアプリをインストールしています。
   (a / am / application / I / installing / Mac / my / new / now / on).

3. たくさんの人がお金を支払うのに電子マネーを使っています。
   (bills / e-money / many / pay / people / to / use).

4. たった今空港に到着して、パソコンを充電しています。
   (airport / am / and / arrived / at / charging / I / just / my / PC / the).

5. ケイトはスマートフォンを使って、遠隔でエアコンの設定を調節しています。
   (AC / adjusting / her / is / Kate / remotely / smartphone / setting / the / with).

Vocabulary for the topic

Exercise E

次のそれぞれの語句の意味を右の選択肢から選びましょう。

1. save electricity	( )	a.	健康管理
2. consumer	( )	b.	機器
3. healthcare	( )	c.	監視する
4. home appliance	( )	d.	電子マネー
5. device	( )	e.	節電する
6. connect	( )	f.	センサー
7. monitor	( )	g.	監視カメラ
8. sensor	( )	h.	消費者
9. electronic money	( )	i.	家庭用電化製品
10. security camera	( )	j.	接続する

Outline

IoT 製品の機能を説明するパラグラフのアウトラインを作りましょう。IoT 製品は、家電、AV 機器、照明、健康機器など、現在目にすることができるものから一つ取り上げましょう。

主題文（その製品には **3** つの機能があることを表明しましょう）

支持文 **1**（**1** つ目の機能を示しましょう）

支持文 **2**（**2** つ目の機能を示しましょう）

支持文 **3**（**3** つ目の機能を示しましょう）

まとめの文（支持文の **3** つの項目をまとめましょう）

Writing a Paragraph

アウトラインを基にパラグラフの下書きを書いてみましょう。それぞれの支持文にディテールを加えることを忘れないようにしましょう。

UNIT 6 旅のプランを立てよう（Time Order）

　食べ物の好みが人それぞれなように、旅行の目当ても人それぞれです。自然や遺跡など、普段の生活では見ることのできないものを見たり、日常の生活では食べたり飲んだりできないものを味わうなど、様々な目的や楽しみ方が考えられます。人によっては、既に行ったことのあるお気に入りの場所に何回も足を運ぶ人もいます。楽しい旅にするために、事前に十分な情報を集め、しっかりと旅行計画を立てましょう。

Warm Up

A. 次のアンケートに答えましょう。

1. How many times have you traveled abroad?

　　□ 1-3 times　　　　　　　　□ 4-6 times
　　□ over 7 times　　　　　　□ I've never been abroad.

2. Do you prefer to travel by car, train, or plane?

　　□ car　　　　　　　　　　□ train
　　□ plane　　　　　　　　　□ other (　　　　　　　　　　)

3. What would you like to do if you have 3 days off?

　　□ to relax on the beach　　□ to hike in the mountains
　　□ to visit a theme park　　□ other (　　　　　　　　　　)

4. Which country do you want to visit the most?

　　□ U.S.A.　　　　　　　　□ China
　　□ South Korea　　　　　　□ other (　　　　　　　　　　)

5. Who do you like to travel with?

　　□ family　　　　　　　　□ friends
　　□ alone　　　　　　　　　□ other (　　　　　　　　　　)

B. アンケートを基に、ペアで会話をしてみましょう。

Paragraph Analysis

時間的順序のパラグラフ

　主題文の主張を説明するために、時間的な順序に沿って議論を展開する方法です。支持文では、以下に示す順序を表す表現を効果的に用いて、時間的な前後関係を表しましょう。また、支持文に続くディテールでは、それぞれの支持文を少しだけ掘り下げて説明します。その際は、時間的な前後関係を崩さないように構成するよう注意しましょう。

時間的順序のパラグラフで用いられる表現

On the first day, ...　　　On the second day, ...　　　On the third day, ...
First (Firstly), ...　　　Second (Secondly), ...　　　Third (Thirdly), ...
First of all, ...　　To begin with, ...
... is followed by ...　　　Next, ...　　　Lastly, ...

Model Paragraph

A Trip to Southern Wakayama

　The Southern part of Wakayama Prefecture is an ideal place for a three-day trip. On the first day, you should go to see pandas in Sirahama Adventure World. You should go there early to beat the crowds. Spend the next day hiking in the Kumano area. There are lots of beautiful trails where you can enjoy peace and solitude. On the last day, head for the coast of Shirahama. The magnificent scenery on the seaside is easily accessible from many hotels. As you see, this area is a great place for a short vacation.

Exercise A

日本語で空欄を埋めて、モデル・パラグラフの構造を確認しましょう。

主題文の内容

目的地	どのような旅行にふさわしいのか

日程	具体的な場所／活動	留意事項／見どころ
1日目		
2日目		
3日目		

まとめの文の内容

Exercise B

（　　　）内に適切な語を入れて、パラグラフを完成しましょう。

A Gourmet Tour of Seoul

Sampling different local dishes in Seoul will be an amazing experience. To (①   ) with, go to the most popular destination, Myeong-dong area, and try the signature meat dish *samgyeopsal*. Containing meat and vegetables, this dish is very healthy. (②   ) the second day, try traditional Korean food at some street stalls. It may be very casual but this experience will make you really appreciate the atmosphere of Seoul. Finally, your trip to Korea is not complete (③   ) you have tried *samgyetang*. This body-warming dish gives you energy to keep sightseeing late into the night. Korean cuisine is extremely varied, of course, so these three dishes are only a few examples of the culinary pleasures that await you.

Grammar for Writing

助動詞 1 （will, must, have to）

助動詞は、文の意味に話者の気持ちを付け加えます。

1. will ― 現在の強い意志、現在の推量、依頼などの意味を付け加える
   a) I haven't eaten anything since this morning. I will eat some street food there.
   b) Kenta will tell me about the history of the festival.
   c) Will you please share your notebook?

2. must ― 義務・必要性、確信のある推量、禁止（否定形で）などの意味を付け加える
   a) You must keep it a secret.
   b) This must be one of the most powerful typhoons in history.
   c) You mustn't forget what I told you now.

3. have to ― 義務・必要性などの意味を付け加える
   a) You have to speak quietly in the hall.
   b) I don't have to pay for that.

Exercise C

次のそれぞれの文の誤りを訂正しましょう。

1. It will is cloudy this afternoon.

2. Junko show will us the best way to prepare sushi.

3. You musts be careful about safety when travelling abroad.

4. You have to speaking loudly when addressing a large crowd.

5. She don't has to pay tax because it is included in the ticket price.

Exercise D

与えられた単語を並べ替えて、日本語を英語にしましょう。

1. 彼らは渋滞がなければ夜までにはそこに着くだろう。
   (by / get / midnight / there / they / will) if there is no traffic jam on the road.

2. 私たちは映画を見た後で家に帰るつもりです。
   (after / go / home / movie / the / watching / we / will).

3. 遠くの方に大きな雲が見えたら、何分もしないうちに雨が降り出すに違いありません。
   If you see a big cloud in the distance, (a / after / few / it / minutes / must / rain).

4. 外出したら、11時までに帰宅しなければならないことを忘れてはいけません。
   If you go out, remember that (11 p.m. / be / by / home / must / you).

5. その国では、ハイウェイを運転するためには、特別な免許を取得しなければなりません。
   (a / get / have / license / special / to / you) to be able to drive on the highway.

Vocabulary for the topic

Exercise E

次のそれぞれの語句の意味を右の選択肢から選びましょう。

1. food	( )	a.	祭り
2. beverage	( )	b.	山地の
3. festival	( )	c.	食べ物
4. tradition	( )	d.	伝統
5. mountainous	( )	e.	飲み物
6. vital	( )	f.	博物館
7. horse riding	( )	g.	活気のある
8. sightseeing	( )	h.	お土産
9. museum	( )	i.	乗馬
10. souvenir	( )	j.	観光

Outline

あなたが行きたい旅行先について述べるパラグラフのアウトラインを作りましょう。

主題文（目的地を提示し、その旅行を楽しみにしているという気持ちを述べましょう）

> [   ]

支持文 1（最初の（1 日目の）行き先を決めましょう）

> [   ]

支持文 2（次の（2 日目）の行き先を決めましょう）

> [   ]

支持文 3（最後の（3 日目）の行き先を決めましょう）

> [   ]

まとめの文（主題文を言い換えるか、支持文の 3 つの項目をまとめましょう）

> [   ]

Writing a Paragraph

　アウトラインを基にパラグラフの下書きを書いてみましょう。それぞれの支持文にディテールを加えることを忘れないようにしましょう。ディテールにはそれぞれの場所で何をしたいのか書きましょう。

UNIT 7 コンビニ商品を分類しよう（Classification）

　コンビニエンスストアは街のいたるところにあって、私たちの生活に欠かせないものになっています。弁当コーナーや飲み物コーナー、文房具コーナーなど、商品はコーナーごとに配置されていますが、同じ棚の上に置かれていても、もっと細かく分類することができます。例えば、飲み物は、炭酸飲料・果実飲料・コーヒー飲料などに分けられます。どんな種類の商品があって、それぞれどんな特徴を持っているのか分類しながら考えてみましょう。

Warm Up

A. 次のアンケートに答えましょう。

1. What do you usually buy at a convenience store?
   - ☐ beverages
   - ☐ magazines
   - ☐ boxed lunches
   - ☐ other (　　　　　　　　　　)

2. What kind of sweets do you like best?
   - ☐ Chinese sweets
   - ☐ Western sweets
   - ☐ Japanese sweets
   - ☐ other (　　　　　　　　　　)

3. What type of detergent do you use at home?
   - ☐ liquid detergent
   - ☐ gel detergent
   - ☐ powder detergent
   - ☐ other (　　　　　　　　　　)

4. What kind of adhesive tape do you use when you pack something into a cardboard box?
   - ☐ craft paper tape
   - ☐ plastic tape
   - ☐ cloth tape
   - ☐ other (　　　　　　　　　　)

5. Which type of juice do you usually buy?
   - ☐ canned juice
   - ☐ juice boxes
   - ☐ plastic bottled juice
   - ☐ glass bottled juice

B. アンケートを基に、ペアで会話をしてみましょう。

Paragraph Analysis

分類のパラグラフ

　トピックとして取り上げる項目を、ある一定の基準で分類し説明していく展開方法です。主題文でトピックと分類基準を示し、支持文では分類されたグループごとに説明していいきます。ディテールではグループを構成する要素の具体例を挙げたり、補足説明を加えたりします。

分類のパラグラフで用いられる表現

... can be divided into three groups based on ...
... can be categorized into three groups according to ...
The first / second / last group consists of ...
... belongs to this category.
This group includes ...

Model Paragraph

Newspapers in Convenience Stores

　Newspapers you can find in convenience stores can be divided into three groups based on the main focus of the news. The first group consists of newspapers that cover almost everything. This group includes The Asahi Shimbun, The Yomiuri Shimbun, The Mainichi Shimbun, and other mainstream publications. The second group is made up of newspapers that mainly cover sports. Tokyo Sports, Daily Sports, Nikkan Sports, are included in this group. The third group consists of newspapers that deal with horse racing. This group includes Keiba Eight, Keiba Book, and Kachi-uma. In short, newspapers in convenience stores appeal to a wide range of customers.

Exercise A

日本語で空欄を埋めて、モデル・パラグラフの構造を確認しましょう。

主題文の内容

トピック	分類数	基準

	各グループの説明（支持文）	具体例（ディテール）
第1グループ		
第2グループ		
第3グループ		

まとめの文の内容

Exercise B

（　　　）内に適切な語を入れて、パラグラフを完成しましょう。

Types of Ice Cream

🎧 11

Ice cream can be (① 　　　　　　　　　) into three types based on the amount of milk ingredients. The first type, labelled as "ice cream," must contain at least 15% of milk fat. This group includes Pino, Parm, and Häagen-Dazs. The (② 　　　　　　　) type is "ice milk," with no less than 10% of milk fat. Yukimi Daifuku, Panapp, and Mona-oh are popular varieties in this group. The (③ 　　　　　　) type is called 'lacto ice," which contains at least 3% of milk fat. Essel Super Cup, Soh, Shirokuma, are all examples of "lacto ice". In (④ 　　　　　　), ice cream is just a common name for different types of frozen desserts.

Grammar for Writing

助動詞 2 （can, may）

助動詞は、文の意味に話者の気持ちを付け加えます。

can ― 能力・可能、可能性・推量などの意味を付け加える
- a) I can speak Korean, but I can't write it.
- b) Forced overtime can be a negative result.
- c) It can't be a wolf. Wolves have all died out in Japan.

may ― 確信のない推量や許可などの意味を付け加える
- a) Ted may be in a meeting.
- b) Kate may not want to see me.
- c) "May I borrow your pen?" "Yes, you may."

Exercise C

次のそれぞれの文の誤りを訂正しなさい。

1. The milk tastes strange. It may is spoiled.

2. Can buy I academic books at a convenience store?

3. Vegetables can grouped in a number of different ways.

4. You don't may consider coffee a kind of soft drinks.

5. The whole city lost power. The convenience stores can stay open.

Exercise D

与えられた単語を並べ替えて、日本語を英語にしなさい。

1. この分類は重要かもしれない。
   (be / classification / important / this / may).

   _____

2. これらのケーキの中からひとつ選ぶことができます。
   (cakes / can / choose / of / one / these / you).

   _____

3. 男性用靴下をいくつかのタイプに分類することができます。
   (can / classify / into / men's / several / socks / types / you).

   _____

4. あのコンビニでボールペンを買うことができます。
   (a / at / ball-point / can / convenience / buy / pen / store / that / you).

   _____

5. 何らかの身分証がなければタバコを買うことはできません。
   (buy / cigarettes / identification / may / not / some / without / you).

   _____

Vocabulary for the topic

Exercise E

次のそれぞれの語句の意味を右の選択肢から選びなさい。

1. stationery	( )		a.	中華まん
2. energy drink	( )		b.	化粧品
3. Chinese steamed bun	( )		c.	冷凍食品
4. salad	( )		d.	栄養ドリンク
5. yogurt	( )		e.	乳飲料
6. milk beverage	( )		f.	芳香剤
7. electric bulb	( )		g.	ヨーグルト
8. cosmetics	( )		h.	文房具
9. air refresher	( )		i.	サラダ
10. frozen food	( )		j.	電球

Outline

　コンビニの商品を分類するパラグラフのアウトラインを作りましょう。商品はコンビニで売っているものであれば何でも構いませんが、下位区分ができるようにやや大き目なくくりから選びましょう。

主題文（ある商品が 3 つのグループに分けることができるということと、その分類基準を述べましょう）

　　　　支持文 1（1 つ目のグループの説明をしましょう）

　　　　支持文 2（2 つ目のグループの説明をしましょう）

　　　　支持文 3（3 つ目のグループの説明をしましょう）

まとめの文（支持文の 3 つの項目をまとめましょう）

Writing a Paragraph

　アウトラインを基にパラグラフの下書きを書いてみましょう。それぞれの支持文にディテールを加えることを忘れないようにしましょう。

UNIT 8

モノの新・旧を比べてみよう
(Comparison and Contrast)

　技術革新は、様々な分野で日々私たちの生活様式を変化させています。少し前の時代には考えられなかったほど、便利な暮らしをすることができるようになりました。携帯電話によって世界のどこにいても友だちの声を聞いたり顔を見たりできるようになり、飛行機によってこれまで何日もかかっていた場所に数時間で行けるようになりました。しかしながら、便利さと引き換えに失われたものも忘れてはなりません。何が得られ、何が失われたのか考えてみましょう。

Part II

Warm Up

A. 次のアンケートに答えましょう。

1. How many electronic devices, such as a smartphone, do you own?
   - ☐ 1-3 items
   - ☐ over 7 items
   - ☐ 4-6 items
   - ☐ none

2. Which do you prefer, digital devices or analogue devices, or both?
   - ☐ digital ones
   - ☐ both
   - ☐ analogue ones
   - ☐ it depends

3. What type of technology are you mostly interested in?
   - ☐ AI (artificial intelligence)
   - ☐ wireless technology
   - ☐ driverless cars
   - ☐ other (　　　　　　　　　　)

4. Where are most of your tech products made?
   - ☐ Japan
   - ☐ China
   - ☐ the U.S.
   - ☐ other (　　　　　　　　　　)

5. Which do you think is the most important invention in history?
   - ☐ a wheel
   - ☐ a computer
   - ☐ a light bulb
   - ☐ other (　　　　　　　　　　)

B. アンケートを基に、ペアで会話をしてみましょう。

Paragraph Analysis

比較・対比のパラグラフ

　主題文の主張を説明するために、似たものや対極にあるものを比べて、主張をより明確にする方法です。支持文では、以下に示す比較や対比を表す表現を効果的に用いて、両者の特徴を際立たせましょう。また、支持文に続くディテールでは、それぞれの支持文について調べた情報などを加えましょう。

比較・対比のパラグラフで用いられる表現

Like / Unlike / Similar to / Compared to ...

On the one hand, ..., but on the other hand, ...

However, ...　　Nevertheless, ...　　In contrast, ...　　Conversely, ...

Although/Though ..., ...　　While ..., ...　　Whereas ..., ...

Model Paragraph

Digital or Paper Books?

　E-books have become more popular than paper books because of a number of advantages. One difference is portability. Unlike paper books, e-books take up no physical space and you can carry around your entire library in your backpack. Another difference is cost. In many cases, e-books are cheaper than the paper ones: sometimes they are completely free. Finally, downloading an e-book takes just a few minutes. On the other hand, buying a paperback requires a trip to a bookstore or waiting a few days for delivery. No wonder, more and more people are using e-books these days.

Exercise A

日本語で空欄を埋めて、モデル・パラグラフの構造を確認しましょう。

主題文の内容

比較の観点	電子書籍	紙の書籍
①		
②		
③		

まとめの文の内容

Exercise B

（　　　　）内に適切な語を入れて、パラグラフを完成しましょう。

Vinyl Records and Digital Music

Vinyl records are enjoying a renewed popularity among young Japanese. First, the sound quality is often better (①　　　　　) to digital recordings. Surprisingly, there are still certain sounds which cannot be reproduced by digital technologies. Secondly, (②　　　　　) digital music which is often downloaded and stored on your laptop, vinyl records come in beautiful packaging. You can use record jackets to decorate your home. Finally, some music is not available digitally. On the (③　　　　　) hand, you can enjoy it by buying an old-fashioned vinyl record. Considering these reasons it is no wonder that vinyl records are making a comeback!

助動詞 3 （would, could, might）

助動詞の過去形は時制の一致による用法の他、現在・過去・未来の様々な意味を表します。

1. would — 過去の不規則な習慣、過去の強い意志、丁寧な依頼などを表す
   a) I would sometimes listen to reggae music with my friends.
   b) Jake wouldn't follow his teacher's advice.
   c) Would you come with me to the party tonight?

2. could — 過去の能力・可能、可能性・推量、丁寧な依頼などを表す
   a) I could speak Italian when I was a child.
   b) Kerry could be at a meeting or in his office.
   c) Could you repeat that?

3. might — 確信のない推量や許可などを表す
   a) He might have some difficulty in finding his conclusion.
   b) Might I have a few words with you?

Exercise C

次のそれぞれの文の誤りを訂正しましょう。

1. In ancient era before Shingen, some rivers could overflow their banks every year.

2. When I was a child, nothing can be done without using cables.

3. He asked me if it may be ok to delete the earlier version of the software.

4. That inventor will often experiment with his brother at home those days.

5. Can I listen to this recording using my PC?　Yes, of course you could.

Exercise D

与えられた単語を並べ替えて、日本語を英語にしましょう。

1. ひょっとしたら、技術の進歩には好ましい影響だけではなく悪影響もあるかもしれません。
   Technological innovation (as / as / effects / have / might / negative / positive / well).

2. その会社は、昨年発売したばかりの新型車の問題点を認めようとしなかった。
   (admit / company / not / problems / the / the / would) with the new car model released just last year.

3. 数年前には、ほとんどの人々はこの最新機器を手にすることすらできなかった。
   (advanced / could / equipment / even / get / most / not / people / this) a few years ago.

4. これらの３つの製品の主な違いを説明してもらってもよろしいでしょうか。
   (could / differences / explain / key / the / you) between these three products?

5. このソフトの初期モデルは機能が本当に限られていました。
   Early versions of this software (functions / have / limited / often / very / would).

Vocabulary for the topic

Exercise E

次のそれぞれの語の意味を右の選択肢から選びましょう。

1. conventional ( )	a. 発明家
2. former ( )	b. 革新
3. generation ( )	c. 信号
4. fashion ( )	d. 機器
5. innovation ( )	e. かつての、昔の
6. inventor ( )	f. 伝統的な、従来の
7. latest ( )	g. 可動性の
8. mobile ( )	h. 最新の
9. equipment ( )	i. 流行
10. signal ( )	j. 世代

Outline

技術革新によって変化したモノについてその新旧を比べるパラグラフのアウトラインを作りましょう。

主題文（技術革新で生まれたモノを提示し、それがもたらした変化を述べましょう）

> [空欄]

支持文 1（1 つ目の以前（のモノ）との違いを述べましょう）

> [空欄]

支持文 2（2 つ目の以前（のモノ）との違いを述べましょう）

> [空欄]

支持文 3（3 つ目の以前（のモノ）との違いを述べましょう）

> [空欄]

まとめの文（主題文を別の言葉で言い換えるか、支持文の 3 つの項目をまとめましょう）

> [空欄]

Writing a Paragraph

　アウトラインを基にパラグラフの下書きを書いてみましょう。それぞれの支持文にディテールを加えることを忘れないようにしましょう。

UNIT 9

ソーシャルメディアの影響を考えよう
（Cause and Effect）

ソーシャルメディアは、インターネットを利用してユーザー同士が情報交換をすることを可能にするメディアのことで、SNS（Twitter、Instagram など）や動画共有サイト（YouTube, ニコニコ動画など）、メッセージングアプリ（LINE, WhatsApp など）、などを含みます。それらは私たちの生活に欠かせないものになっており、人間関係のあり方にも変化を起こしています。それぞれのメディアがどのような影響をもたらしているのか考えてみましょう。

Part II

Warm Up

A. 次のアンケートに答えましょう。

1. What type of social media do you use most often?
   - ☐ SNS
   - ☐ messaging applications
   - ☐ video-sharing websites
   - ☐ other（　　　　　　　　　）

2. Which SNS do you think is the most convenient?
   - ☐ Facebook
   - ☐ Twitter
   - ☐ Instagram
   - ☐ mixi

3. Which application do you think is the most popular in Japan?
   - ☐ YouTube
   - ☐ niconico
   - ☐ TwistCasting
   - ☐ other（　　　　　　　　）

4. Who are most influenced by YouTube?
   - ☐ teenagers
   - ☐ young adults
   - ☐ elderly people
   - ☐ other（　　　　　　　　）

5. How many hours a day do you spend using social media?
   - ☐ an hour
   - ☐ two hours
   - ☐ three hours
   - ☐ other（　　　　　　　　）

B. アンケートを基に、ペアで会話をしてみましょう。

原因と結果のパラグラフ

　主題文で原因を示し、支持文でその原因がもたらす結果や影響を提示・説明していく展開方法です。ここでは、3つの支持文を展開しますので、1つの原因に対して3つの結果や影響を述べることになります。ディテールではそれぞれの結果を補足説明します。

原因と結果のパラグラフで用いられる表現

　<u>　原因　</u>　cause / lead to / result in　<u>　結果・影響　</u>
　<u>　原因　</u>　influence / have an effect on / contribute to　<u>　結果・影響　</u>
　<u>　原因　</u>　help (to) do / help 人 (to) do
　Because of / As a result of / Due to / Thanks to　<u>　原因　</u>,　<u>　結果・影響　</u>

Model Paragraph

The Benefits of Advertising on SNS

　　Advertising on a Social Network Service (SNS) can be very effective for business. First, it helps to spread information very quickly. Once you upload the details about a product or a service, the information reaches millions of people. Second, it can reduce advertising costs. Ads on SNS are much cheaper than traditional ads. Third, it can help build brand loyalty among young consumers. Young people around the world rely on SNS for the latest news, rather than on TV or newspapers. In conclusion, SNS advertising produces results by rapidly spreading information at a limited cost and building brand loyalty.

Exercise A

日本語で空欄を埋めて、モデル・パラグラフの構造を確認しましょう。

主題文の内容

原因	効果の対象

支持文

効果 1	
効果 2	
効果 3	

まとめの文の内容

Exercise B

（　　　）内に適切な語を入れて、パラグラフを完成しましょう。

The Impact of SNS on Young People

Excessive use of SNS can (①　　　　　　　　　　) a negative impact on the mental health of young people. First, it can cause anxiety. Some people may feel depressed when they see pictures of others enjoying themselves. Secondly, overuse of SNS can (②　　　　　　　　　　) sleep problems. It is difficult to fall asleep after spending a lot of time staring at the computer screen. Third, it can cause FOMO, (③　　　　　　　　　) the "Fear of Missing Out". Young people are reluctant to put down their smartphones out of fear that they will miss something important. (④　　　　　　　　) short, to avoid serious health issues, SNS should be used in moderation.

Grammar for Writing

等位接続詞

　文法上対等な関係にある語と語、句と句、節と節を結びつける接続詞を等位接続詞といいます。and, but, or などが代表的な例です。

1. 語と語

   Baby pandas are sweet and lovely.

   My room is small but comfortable.

2. 句と句

   I enjoyed playing tennis and watching TV yesterday.

   Is Mary at home or at the office?

3. 節と節

   You can take a train to Sapporo, or you can fly there.

   I was born in London, but I live in Sydney now.

Exercise C

次のそれぞれの文の誤りを訂正しましょう。

1. Twitter is very useful and convenience.

2. I just listen to music and watching music videos on YouTube.

3. I use a smartphone to write e-mails. But my father uses a computer.

4. Facebook and Twitter and Instagram are examples of SNS.

5. On this site, you can ask questions but write comments related to the recent news.

Exercise D

与えられた単語を並べ替えて、日本語を英語にしましょう。

1. 私たちの会社は商品の販売促進のために、ツイッターとフェイスブックを使っています。
   (and / company / Facebook / our / our / products / promote / to / Twitter / uses).

2. ウィキペディアは役に立ちますが、必ずしも信用できるとは限りません。
   (always / but / is / not / reliable / useful / Wikipedia).

3. ソーシャルメディアを通して、プライベート写真をアップロードしたり共有したりできます。
   (and / can / media / photos / private / share / social / through / upload / you).

4. 私はフェイスブックにメッセージを投稿しましたが、誰も返事をしてくれませんでした。
   (a / but / Facebook / I / it /message / nobody / on / posted / replied / to).

5. このアプリはユーザーが生放送を流したり、見たりすることを可能にします。
   (allows / and / application / broadcasts / live / stream / this / to / users / watch).

Vocabulary for the topic

Exercise E

次のそれぞれの語句の意味を右の選択肢から選びましょう。

1. account ( )
2. share ( )
3. personal information ( )
4. cyberbullying ( )
5. app ( )
6. live stream ( )
7. online fraud ( )
8. Q and A site ( )
9. educational content ( )
10. data breach ( )

a. 教育的コンテンツ
b. アプリ
c. アカウント
d. オンライン詐欺
e. データ漏洩
f. 共有する
g. 生配信
h. ネットいじめ
i. 個人情報
j. 質疑応答サイト

Outline

　代表的なソーシャルメディアを取り上げて、その影響を説明するパラグラフのアウトラインを作りましょう。取り上げるソーシャルメディアは SNS、動画共有サイト、メッセージングアプリなどの大きな枠組みでも、Facebook, YouTube, LINE のように個別のサービスでも良いです。

主題文（取り上げるソーシャルメディアが、誰(何)に対して、肯定的あるいは否定的な影響を与えるのか表明しましょう。）

```



```

支持文 1（1 つ目の影響を示しましょう）

```



```

支持文 2（2 つ目の影響を示しましょう）

```



```

支持文 3（3 つ目の影響を示しましょう）

```



```

まとめの文（主題文を別の言葉で言い換えましょう）

```



```

Writing a Paragraph

　アウトラインを基にパラグラフの下書きを書いてみましょう。それぞれの支持文にディテールを加えることを忘れないようにしましょう。

UNIT 10 大学生の健康問題を解決しよう（Problem-Solution）

　高校生の時とは異なり、大学生になると自由な時間が増え、自分で決めなければならないことも多くなります。それに伴って、健康面も自分で責任を持って管理しなければなりません。飲酒や運動不足など高校生のころにはあまり考えなかったことにも多くの健康問題が潜んでいます。大学生の健康問題をどのように解決したら良いか考えてみましょう。

Warm Up

A. 次のアンケートに答えましょう。

1. How often do you usually eat breakfast?
   - ☐ 1-3 times a week
   - ☐ every day
   - ☐ 4-6 times a week
   - ☐ I never eat breakfast.

2. Do you enjoy snacking between meals?
   - ☐ every day
   - ☐ not really
   - ☐ often enough
   - ☐ never

3. Do you enjoy vegetables?
   - ☐ yes, eat them daily
   - ☐ not really
   - ☐ on occasion
   - ☐ never

4. How many hours do you sleep a day?
   - ☐ 1-4 hours
   - ☐ 7-8 hours
   - ☐ 5-6 hours
   - ☐ more than 8 hours

5. How many hours a day do you use your smartphone?
   - ☐ less than 1 hour
   - ☐ 3-4 hours
   - ☐ 1-2 hours
   - ☐ more than 4 hours

B. アンケートを基に、ペアで会話をしてみましょう。

Paragraph Analysis

問題解決のパラグラフ

　主題文の主張を説明するために、解決方法を議論していく方法です。支持文では、以下に示す解決方法を紹介する表現を効果的に用いて、問題との関係性を表しましょう。また、支持文に続くディテールでは、それぞれの解決方法について、それを取り上げた根拠となるような情報を追加して説明します。

問題解決のパラグラフで用いられる表現

According to …, …　　　As … point(s) out / indicate(s) / suggest(s), …

… help(s) … (to) *do*　　　… make(s) A B　　　… give(s) AB

It can be presumed that …　　　It is suggested that …

モデル・パラグラフ

Overcoming Insomnia

　There are several ways for university students to overcome their frequent problem of insomnia. One idea is to get regular exercise. Studies have shown that physical exercise has a positive effect on the quality of sleep. Going to bed at a regular hour is also important. According to medical reports, if you go to bed around the same time every night, you will fall asleep more easily. Finally, make sure that your bedroom is not too hot. This is especially important in the summer. Good sleep is necessary in order to have a healthy life.

Exercise A

日本語で空欄を埋めて、モデル・パラグラフの構造を確認しましょう。

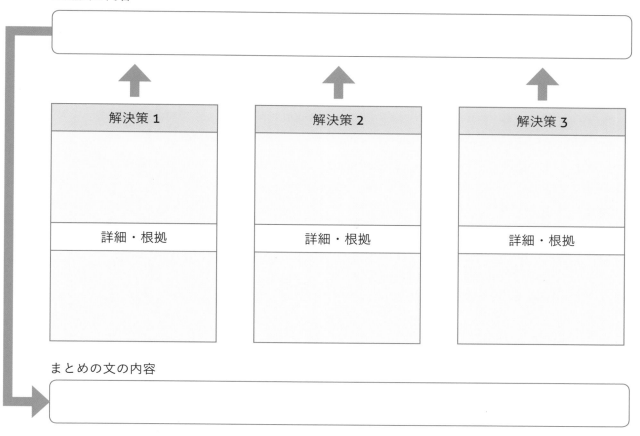

主題文の内容

解決策 1	解決策 2	解決策 3
詳細・根拠	詳細・根拠	詳細・根拠

まとめの文の内容

Exercise B

（　　　　　）内に適切な語を入れて、パラグラフを完成しましょう。

Eating Habits

In order to maintain a healthy lifestyle, university students need to improve their eating habits. First of all, you should never skip breakfast. The first meal of the day (① ＿＿＿＿＿＿＿＿) us the necessary energy to function effectively throughout the day. Secondly, make sure to eat enough vegetables. (② ＿＿＿＿＿＿＿＿) to many scientific studies, raw vegetables are an important source of vitamins. Finally, establish a regular eating routine. Don't have a large dinner just before going to bed and avoid snacks between meals. These rules are pretty easy to follow and help you maintain a healthy and enjoyable (③ ＿＿＿＿＿＿＿＿).

Grammar for Writing

従位接続詞

　主節と従属節とを結びつける接続詞で、従属節に名詞や副詞などの機能をもたせます。とりわけ副詞節の用法は多様で、時、場所、原因、理由、目的、結果、条件、譲歩などがあります。

1. 名詞節を導く接続詞 — that, if, whether など。
   a) It surprises me that he doesn't eat vegetables at all.
   b) It is true that we need at least 7 hours of sleep per night to function well.
   c) Whether the new model will be released will be announced on Friday.

2. 副詞節を導く接続詞 — when, where, while, because, since, as, that, if, unless, than など
   a) If you smoke, you are more at risk of developing cancer.
   b) Unless your doctor tells you otherwise, you should try to exercise a few days a week.

3. 目的や条件を表す語句 — so that, in order that, in case, as long as
   a) Eat vegetables regularly so that you can have a proper vitamin intake.
   b) In case you get sick on the trip, bring some painkillers.
   c) Any sport will do as long as you move your body.

Exercise C

次のそれぞれの文の誤りを指摘しましょう。

1. We will know tonight if or not he has influenza.

2. My manager has stated very clearly whether we should not work overtime.

3. That few university students take insomnia seriously, it can have very negative health effects.

4. Many university students can sleep as long as want to.

5. Since all the people in the building woke up, the noise outside was so loud.

Exercise D

与えられた単語を並べ替えて、日本語を英語にしましょう。

1. 病気になるか健康のままでいるかは、生活習慣にかかっている。
   (we / healthy / get / stay / whether / sick / or) depends on our lifestyle.

   _____

2. あなたが実家にいる間は、両親が大いに助けてくれるでしょう。
   (you / at / are / while / home / living), your parents will really help you.

   _____

3. スイーツを食べすぎたので太ってしまった。
   (eating / I / sweets / been / much / since / too / have), I've gained weight.

   _____

4. 筋力を強くするために、規則的な運動をしましょう。
   Make sure to get regular exercise (that / strength / gain / you / so / muscle).

   _____

5. 肺ガンのリスクを減らしたければ、タバコはやめるべきです。
   You should stop smoking (if / you / to / want / the / minimize / risk) of lung cancer.

   _____

Vocabulary for the topic

Exercise E

次のそれぞれの語句の意味を右の選択肢から選びましょう。

1. nutrition	( )	a.	バランス
2. fat	( )	b.	アルバイト
3. alcohol	( )	c.	栄養
4. smoking	( )	d.	運動
5. lifestyle	( )	e.	脂肪
6. fatigue	( )	f.	視力
7. part-time job	( )	g.	生活習慣
8. balance	( )	h.	アルコール
9. exercise	( )	i.	喫煙
10. eyesight	( )	j.	疲労

Outline

大学生の健康問題の解決策について述べるパラグラフのアウトラインを作りましょう。

主題文（大学生の健康について、何が問題なのかを主張しましょう）

>

支持文1（1つ目の解決方法を書きましょう）

>

支持文2（2つ目の解決方法を書きましょう）

>

支持文3（3つめの解決方法を書きましょう）

>

まとめの文（主題文を別の言葉で言い換えるか、支持文の3つの解決策をまとめましょう）

>

Writing a Paragraph

　アウトラインを基にパラグラフの下書きを書いてみましょう。それぞれの支持文にディテールを加えることを忘れないようにしましょう。

パラグラフからプレゼンテーションへ 1（Introduction）

　「おしゃべり」とは違って、プレゼンテーションには構造があります。この Part では、まず聴衆に正しく効率的に内容を伝えるための一般的なプレゼンテーションの構造を学びます。また、実際に導入（Introduction）を作成します。

プレゼンテーションの構造

　以下の図は、わかりやすいプレゼンテーションの基本構造です。これまでに学んできたパラグラフの基本構造と似ていることを確かめましょう。

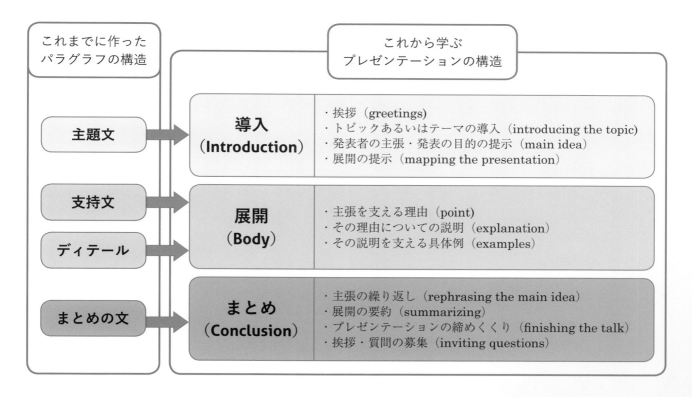

プレゼンテーションの基本構造が果たす役割

　わかりやすいプレゼンテーションをするために大切なことは何でしょうか。声の大きさや提示資料ももちろん大切ですが、それ以前に発表者と聴衆がプレゼンテーションの基本構造をお互いに理解していることが重要です。共通理解の基本構造に基づいて発表すれば、考えたことを効率よく聴衆に伝えることができます。

Good morning, everyone. I'm happy to have an opportunity to speak to you today. My presentation today is about a health issue which is a concern for many university students. The purpose of this presentation is to offer some ideas regarding the problem of lack of sleep for those who begin to live alone. In my brief presentation I will outline three possible solutions to tackle this problem. So, let's move on to how you can maintain a healthy sleeping pattern.

First of all, in order to sleep well, you should get regular exercise. Jogging, swimming or just taking a walk has a very positive effect on our overall physical health. According to numerous academic studies, moderate exercise on a daily basis contributes to the quality of sleep. Another way to improve your sleep pattern is to make sure that you go to bed at a regular hour. According to medical reports, if you go to bed around the same time every night, you will fall asleep more easily. Even if you have a lot of assignments, try getting up a bit earlier instead of staying up late. Finally, make sure that your bedroom is not too hot. Many scientific reports suggest that we fall asleep faster in a cool room and enjoy a more restful sleep. This is especially important in the hot summer months.

In conclusion, good sleep is necessary in order to have a productive and healthy life. Today I described three steps you can take to improve the quality of your sleep: exercise, go to bed at a regular hour and keep your room cool at night. That concludes my speech and I will take any questions you may have.

「導入」の構造

　導入では、プレゼンテーション全体を聞くのに必要な情報を聴衆に提示します。ここの出来栄えで、プレゼンテーション全体で自分が言いたいことがうまく伝わるかどうかが決まります。導入の構成要素としては以下のようなものがあります。

1. 挨拶（greetings）

　　まずは発表者と聴衆との信頼関係を築くことが重要です。時間帯や立場を踏まえたことばを適切に選択し、聴衆との信頼関係を築きましょう。

2. トピックの導入（introducing the topic）

　　次に説明する「発表者の主張」を効果的に聴衆に伝えるためにも、これから何について話すかをあらかじめ提示します。

3. 発表者の主張・発表の目的の提示（main idea）

　　発表を通して最も言いたいことを述べます。パラグラフ・ライティングにおける主題文に当たる部分です。後の Exercise では、皆さんが Unit 10 で作成したパラグラフの主題文を利用して作成してもらいます。

4. 展開の提示（mapping the presentation）

　　プレゼンテーションの展開を簡単にまとめます。聴衆は「これからプレゼンテーションがどんな順番で進んでいくのか」を知り、内容を把握しやすくなります。

以下の (1) 〜 (6) の文が導入のどの要素に当てはまるのか、前頁の説明を参考に答えましょう。

(1) Good morning, everyone. (2) I'm happy to have an opportunity to speak to you

1.		2.

today. (3) My presentation today is about a health issue which is a concern for many

3.

university students. (4) The purpose of this presentation is to offer some ideas regarding

4.

the problem of lack of sleep for those who begin to live alone. (5) In my brief presentation

5.

I will outline three possible solutions to tackle this problem. (6) So, let's move on to how

6.

you can maintain a healthy sleeping pattern.

Language for Presentation

プレゼンテーションの導入では次のような表現がよく使われます。

1. 挨拶
   Hello, everyone.
   Good morning, ladies and gentlemen.
   I'm happy to have an opportunity to make this presentation here today.

2. トピックの導入
   Today, I'd like to talk about ...
   In this presentation, I'd like to focus on ...
   My presentation today is about ...
   The key objective of this presentation is ...

3. 発表者の主張・発表の目的の提示
   The most important point in my presentation is ...
   I will argue that ...

4. 展開の提示

In my brief presentation, I will describe three possible factors.

My talk is divided into three parts.

In my speech I will focus on three main elements.

Vocabulary for Presentation

次のそれぞれの語の意味を右の選択肢から選びましょう。

1.	focus	(	)	a.	主張する
2.	divide	(	)	b.	構成
3.	compose	(	)	c.	部分
4.	element	(	)	d.	挨拶
5.	opportunity	(	)	e.	機会
6.	subject	(	)	f.	主題
7.	greeting	(	)	g.	要素
8.	part	(	)	h.	構成する
9.	structure	(	)	i.	分ける
10.	argue	(	)	j.	焦点

Your Own Presentation

Unit 10 で作成したパラグラフの主題文をもとに、導入の原稿を完成しましょう。

挨拶：

トピックの導入：

発表者の主張・発表の目的の提示：

展開の提示：

Grammar for Presentation

名詞および形容詞

1. 名詞：加算名詞と不加算名詞がある

普通名詞 – すべて可算名詞

    a) Apples are fruits. An apple is a fruit.

    b) I like apples.

    c) He goes to school by bus.

固有名詞、集合名詞、物質名詞、抽象名詞

    d) The audience was very small. Her audience were all quiet.

    e) There are three sheets of paper.

    f) He gave me important information.

2. 形容詞：原則として名詞の前に置かれて名詞を修飾する

    a) The beautiful little white rose reminded me of my cousin's visit.

    b) The highway was long, windy and pretty boring.

Exercise B

次のそれぞれの文の誤りを訂正しましょう。

1. You can get many useful information from this webpage.
2. The policemen is investigating the details of the traffic accident.
3. A pollution is one of the biggest problems our society is facing today.
4. It is amazed that some athletes can run a full marathon in under two hours.
5. The patient will feel much good soon.

Exercise C

与えられた単語を並べ替えて、日本語を英語にしましょう。

1. 君が警察に情報を提供すればするほど事件は解決に向かうだろう。

(the / information / more / provide / you), the quicker the case will be solved.

2. 国によっては、酒類の販売を厳格に禁止している場合がある。

(sale / countries / the / strictly / some / alcohol / control / of).

3. 消費税が上がれば、貧しい人々に悪影響があるでしょう。

If the consumption tax goes up, (will / poor / have / it / on / negative / a / effect / the).

4. 規則正しい睡眠は記憶力の向上につながるかもしれない。

(sleep / our / memory / improve / may / regular).

5. 黒い瞳のきれいな女の子を覚えている。

(girl / eyes / beautiful / I / dark / a / with / remember).

Part III

　効果的なプレゼンテーションを行うためには、内容がよく整理されていて言語面でも洗練されていることが大切なのは言うまでもありませんが、視覚的な提示資料を用いることで聴衆への意味伝達がスムーズになる場合があります。

　視覚資料の作成には、大学生にもおなじみの Microsoft 社の PowerPoint のほかにも、Keynote、Prezi など、たくさんのソフトウェアを利用することができます。自分に合ったソフトウェアを見つけて、より良い視覚資料の作成に取り組んでみましょう。このセクションでは、特定のソフトウェアは想定せず、紙芝居の形式で一枚の紙をどのように構成するかを学んでいきます。

導入で用いられるスライド例

　導入で用いられるスライドには、以下の 3 種類が含まれるのが一般的です。

1. **タイトル・氏名・日付**：タイトルでは文頭と 4 文字以上の単語は大文字で始めます
2. **主張**：シンプルな表現で大きな文字で書きます
3. **展開**：箇条書きと適切な字下げで、プレゼンテーションがどう構成されているのか示します

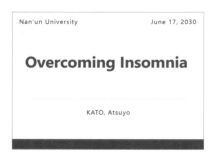

✓Points

◆ **英語での発表に向けた提示資料作りの 8 つのポイント**

- 半角と全角の違いに注意する（全角は用いない）
- Arial や Helvetica などサンセリフ体に属するフォントを用いる
- 文字サイズは統一する
- 文字の色は、基本の色以外には多くても強調するための 2 色程度にとどめる
- アニメーションを用いる場合は最小限にする
- 1 枚のスライドには言いたいことを 1 つまでに抑える
- 原稿をそのまま貼り付けず、キーワードだけのシンプルな表現を用いる
- 文字よりも数字や図やグラフを重視する

UNIT 12 パラグラフからプレゼンテーションへ2（Body）

Unit 11 では、プレゼンテーション全体の基本構造と導入の作り方を学びました。この Unit で扱う展開（Body）は、文章量が多くなりますが似た作業も多いので、コツをつかめばすぐに上達することができます。

「展開」の構造

展開は、導入で述べた発表者の主張に対して、そう考えるに至った理由を論理的に述べる部分です。Part 2 では、1つのパラグラフ内に支持文とディテールの組み合わせを 3 つ作ってきました。その 3 つに対応させる形で、項目①、項目②、項目③の 3 つの部分から成る「展開」を作成します。項目①、②、③のそれぞれに含めるべき要素には以下のようなものがあります。

1. 主張を支える理由（point）

導入で述べた主張を裏付ける理由を述べます。パラグラフ・ライティングにおける支持文に当たる部分です。後の Exercise では、Unit 10 で作成したパラグラフの支持文を利用して作成してもらいます。なお、最初の理由を挙げる前に、これから展開が始まることを述べましょう。また、各項目の間には転換を示す語を用いて、3 つの要素を分かりやすく伝えるようにしましょう。

2. その理由についての説明（explanation）

1 ではできるだけシンプルに要点を伝えるように心がけ、2 では明確に説明しきれなかった部分を補って理由が適切であることを説明しましょう。抽象的な事柄や前提知識が必要な説明には特に補足が必要です。これまでに作ってきたパラグラフのディテールがこれにあたる場合には、それを活用しましょう。

3. その理由を支える具体例（examples）

例を表す表現を用いて、それが具体例であることを聴衆に伝えましょう。これまでに作ってきたパラグラフのディテールがこれにあたる場合には、それを活用しましょう。

以下の (4) 〜 (9) の文が展開のどの要素に当てはまるのか、前ページの説明をもとに答えましょう。

(1) First of all, in order to sleep well, you should get regular exercise. (2) Jogging,

| 1. 主張を支える理由 |

| 2. その理由についての説明 |

swimming or just taking a walk has a very positive effect on our overall physical health.

(3) According to numerous academic studies, moderate exercise on a daily basis

| 3. 理由を支える具体例 |

contributes to the quality of sleep. (4) Another way to improve your sleep pattern is to

| 4. |

make sure that you go to bed at a regular hour. (5) According to medical reports, if you

| 5. |

go to bed around the same time every night, you will fall asleep more easily. (6) Even if

| 6. |

you have a lot of assignments, try getting up a bit earlier instead of staying up late.

(7) Finally, make sure that your bedroom is not too hot. (8) Many scientific reports

| 7. |

| 8. |

suggest that we fall asleep faster in a cool room and enjoy a more restful sleep. (9) This

| 9. |

is especially important in the hot summer months.

Language for Presentation

プレゼンテーションの展開では次のような表現がよく使われます。

1. 主張を支える理由

   First of all, S + V.

   Another way to solve the problem is to do.

   I'm going to share with you the final reason: S + V.

2. その理由についての説明

   It includes ...

   I would like to emphasize that S + V.

   It should be noted that S + V.

3. その理由を支える具体例

   According to media reports, S + V.

   As it is pointed out by ..., S + V.   As ... point(s) out, S + V.

   For example, S + V.   For instance, S + V.

Vocabulary for Presentation

次のそれぞれの語句の意味を右の選択肢から選びましょう。

		( )		
1.	emphasis	( )	a.	示す
2.	solve	( )	b.	～によると
3.	stress	( )	c.	指摘する
4.	include	( )	d.	マスコミ報道
5.	according to	( )	e.	解決する
6.	point out	( )	f.	事例
7.	indicate	( )	g.	学術研究
8.	media report	( )	h.	含む
9.	academic studies	( )	i.	強調
10.	case	( )	j.	強調する

Your Own Presentation

Unit 10 で作成したパラグラフの支持文とディテールを用いて展開の原稿を完成しましょう。

主張を支える理由①：

その理由についての説明①：

その理由を支える具体例①：

主張を支える理由②：

その理由についての説明②：

その理由を支える具体例②：

主張を支える理由③：

その理由についての説明③：

その理由を支える具体例③：

Grammar for Presentation

副詞

副詞は、動詞だけでなく形容詞や他の副詞、文全体も修飾する場合がある。

1. 動詞を修飾する副詞 － 位置の自由度が高い
   a) Suddenly we realized the data was completely wrong.
   b) I usually prepare my presentation before the class.
   c) She delivered her presentation successfully.

2. 形容詞や他の副詞を修飾する副詞 － 原則として被修飾語の近く
   a) His suggestion is very interesting and we want to know more.
   b) They are working pretty hard to meet the deadlines.
   c) The screen was large enough.

3. 文を修飾する副詞
   a) Personally, I agree with you.
   b) Fortunately no one was listening to his joke.

Exercise B

次のそれぞれの文の誤りを訂正しましょう。

1. I don't really think they remember good what happened on that day.
2. You must have heard this story ago.
3. Such measures are necessarily if we want to save the environment.
4. This economic support was great appreciated by the developing countries.
5. Unfortunate, I received his email with the schedule too late and could not join the group.

Exercise C

与えられた単語を並べ替えて、日本語を英語にしましょう。

1. 速やかに保険会社に事故の詳細を知らせましょう。
   (company / insurance / know / let / the) all the details of the accident immediately.
2. 被雇用者の権利は大いに尊重されなければなりません。
   (all / at / be / employees / must / of / respected / rights / time / the / the).
3. 確かに、戦争は国際紛争を解決する手段ではありません。
   (certainly / conflicts / international / is / not / solve / the / to / war / way / ,).
4. 規則正しい睡眠時間を維持することは実際には至って簡単です。
   (actually / easy / hours / is / it / maintain / regular / sleeping / to).
5. 信じられないくらい大きな地震がいつかその島に来るかもしれないと科学者が予測しています。
   Scientists predict that (an / earthquake / hit / incredibly / may / powerful) the island one day.

Visual Aids

　「展開」は文章量が多いので、必要な情報を絞って、文字だらけの視覚資料にならないように工夫しましょう。自分の意見を説得的に伝えるためには、根拠を明確に示すことが大切です。つまり、自分の思い込みや直感にもとづく議論ではなく、主張に至る判断材料がありそれを聞き手に示すということが求められます。視覚資料にはそれらをうまく盛り込む必要があります。

展開で用いられるスライド例

　展開で用いられるスライドには、以下の3種類が含まれるのが一般的です。

1. 主張を支える理由：理由が複数ある場合は適切な連番をつけ、シンプルな表現で書きます
2. その理由についての説明：必要に応じて理由の補足説明を提示します
3. その理由を支える具体例：図表やイラストを用いながら具体例を示します

☑Points

◆ **英語の発表に向けた情報倫理の8つのポイント**

　展開などで具体例や根拠となる情報を示す際には、著作権法をはじめ守るべきルールがあります。

- ・キャラクターや他人の肖像などを無許可で掲載しない
- ・引用した場合にはタイトルやURL等の出典情報を示す
- ・引用した情報には勝手な改訂を加えない
- ・聞いた話等ではなく、新聞・雑誌や公的機関の発行物等の公共性の高い情報源を用いる
- ・間接的な引用は控え、可能な限り原典にあたる
- ・SNSや個人ブログ等の引用は控え、情報源とする際にも根拠をしっかりと確かめる
- ・可能な限り複数の情報源を参照する
- ・人や団体を誹謗中傷する内容は掲載しない

UNIT 13　パラグラフからプレゼンテーションへ3（Conclusion）

Unit 11, Unit 12 では、Unit 10 で作ったパラグラフをもとにプレゼンテーションの導入と展開の作り方を学びました。この Unit では、同様にプレゼンテーションの締めくくりであるまとめ（conclusion）の作り方を学びます。

「まとめ」の構造

まとめでは、導入と展開で述べた内容を短くまとめながら、発表者の主張を再度明確に述べます。展開のところで、主張に対する根拠は既に聴衆と共有しているので、ここで繰り返される主張はより聴衆に伝わりやすくなるはずです。Part 2 で作成したパラグラフのまとめの文をもとにして主張を繰り返し、さらに展開で述べた3つの項目に言及する形式を学びます。まとめに含めるべき要素には以下のようなものがあります。

1. 主張の繰り返し（rephrasing the main idea）

導入で述べた主張を繰り返します。パラグラフ・ライティングのまとめの文に当たる部分です。まとめの文を書く際には、主題文と全く同じ文にならないように注意しました。ここでも、導入での主張と全く同じ表現にならないように、別の角度から同じ内容の主張を述べましょう。また、必ず転換を示す語から始めましょう。

2. 展開の要約（summarizing）

展開で触れた3つの項目を1文程度にまとめます。展開で述べたことの確認に過ぎませんので、シンプルな表現を心がけましょう。

3. プレゼンテーションの締めくくり（finishing the talk）

プレゼンテーションが終了したのか、ただ言葉につまっているのかが分からなければ、発表が台無しです。これで終わりであるということをはっきりと伝えましょう。

4. 挨拶・質問の募集（inviting questions）

はじまりの挨拶で築いた聴衆との距離感を保つうえでも、最後に質問を求めることは重要です。自分の説明で分かりにくかった箇所などを指摘してもらいましょう。

以下の (1) 〜 (3) の文がまとめのどの要素に当てはまるのか、前ページの説明をもとに答えましょう。

(1) In conclusion, good sleep is necessary in order to have a productive and healthy life.

1.

(2) Today I described three steps you can take to improve the quality of your sleep:

2.

exercise, go to bed at a regular hour and keep your room cool at night. (3) That

3.

concludes my speech and I will take any questions you may have.

Language for Presentation

プレゼンテーションのまとめでは次のような表現がよく使われます。

1. 主張の繰り返し
   Therefore, …
   Thus, …
   In conclusion, …
   Consequently, …
   Hence, …

2. 展開の要約
   The main points are as follows: …
   Let me remind you of the issues we have covered. As the issues, we mentioned…

3. プレゼンテーションの締めくくり
   I would like to stop here.
   That concludes my speech.
   That covers everything I'd like to say.
   Thank you for your attention.

4. 挨拶・質問の募集
   Are there any questions?
   Does anyone have any questions or comments?

Vocabulary for Presentation

次のそれぞれの語の意味を右の選択肢から選びましょう。

1. cover	(　　)	a. 意見
2. conclusion	(　　)	b. 思い出させる
3. outline	(　　)	c. 含む、扱う
4. issue	(　　)	d. 注意
5. consequently	(　　)	e. その結果
6. summarize	(　　)	f. 結論付ける
7. comment	(　　)	g. 結論
8. remind	(　　)	h. 論点
9. conclude	(　　)	i. 要約する
10. attention	(　　)	j. 概要を述べる

Your Own Presentation

Unit 10 で作成したパラグラフのまとめの文をもとに、まとめの原稿を完成させましょう。

主張の繰り返し：

展開の要約：

プレゼンテーションの締めくくり：

挨拶・質問の募集：

Grammar for Presentation

命令文（Imperative Sentences）

1. 命令文

   命令文は、主語の you を省略し、動詞の原形から始めるのが基本です。

   a) Look at this graph / table.

   b) Take a close look at this graph / table.

   c) Don't interrupt while a presenter is speaking.

2. 丁寧なニュアンスの命令文

   疑問文を用いて、丁寧なニュアンスの命令を表すことがあります。

   a) Could / Would you give me more information about that?

   b) Would you mind opening the window?

3. let を用いた命令文

   a) Let me explain the situation.

   b) Let us help you conduct your research more efficiently.

Exercise B

次のそれぞれの文の誤りを訂正しましょう。

1. Please raising your hand if you have a question.

2. Don't starting eating until everyone is seated.

3. Doesn't share his proposal with anybody until his presentation is finished.

4. Would you mind help me to carry these materials for the presentation today?

5. Let I give you some more evidence to support my main argument.

与えられた単語を並べ替えて、日本語を英語にしましょう。

1. あまり多くの質問をせず、他の人にもチャンスをあげてください。

   (ask / don't / many / questions / too) and give other people a chance.

   _____

2. 質問に答える前にもう少しだけ考えさせてください。

   (a / about / bit / let / me / more / question / think / your) before answering.

   _____

3. 今回の選挙についてあまり質問しないでいただけますか。

   (any / asking / mind / not / questions / would / you) about the recent election?

   _____

4. あなたの結論を支えるどんな証拠でも教えてください。

   (any / conclusion / evidence / know / let / supports / us / which / your).

   _____

5. 講義がとても面白かったので、彼の新しい本を読んでみたいです。

   As the lecture was very interesting, (book / his / I / latest / love / read / to / would).

   _____

Visual aids

　まとめは、プレゼンテーションの成否を握る大事な部分です。デザイン面にも注意しながら、プレゼンテーション全体の統一感を築き上げましょう。色遣いについては PC 等のディスプレイと印刷物とで大きく異なる場合がありますので、事前にしっかりと確認することが重要です。この Unit では、色遣いを含むデザイン面についての注意点を学んでいきましょう。

まとめで用いられるスライド例

　まとめで用いられるスライドには、以下の 3 種類が含まれるのが一般的です

1. **主張や理由**：1 ～ 2 枚程度で、発表で最も言いたかったことを簡潔にまとめます

2. **引用文献のリスト**：聴衆が同じ情報をたどることができるよう、正確に記します

3. **プレゼンテーションの終わり**：発表が終わったことを示し、質問の募集や連絡先を提示します

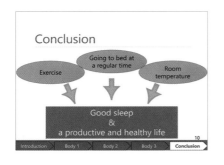 

Thank you for your attention!

☑ Points

　◆ 英語の発表に向けたスライドデザインの 8 つのポイント

- スライドの中の色は、背景色、文字の基本色、タイトルや小見出しなどの色、強調の色の 4 色ぐらいまでにする
- 4 色の使い方には一定の規則性を持たせ、全体を通して一貫した色遣いにする
- 背景色は印刷するときのことも考えて、白を基本とする
- 文字の基本色は、背景色が白であれば、黒やグレーにすると読みやすい
- タイトル（またはタイトルの背景）や小見出しの色は、落ち着いた色にして、全ページで統一する
- 強調の色は他で使う色とは異なる派手目の色がよい→赤やオレンジが効果的
- タイトルや強調などで文字の背景に色を付ける場合は、ハレーション（明るい色の組み合わせで目がチカチカする現象）を起こさないように注意する
- 画像やイラストが文字の色と干渉し合わないように注意する

UNIT 14 プレゼンテーションの評価（Evaluation）

これまでの Unit で作ったプレゼンテーションを自分たちで評価してみましょう。評価の方法は二つあって、自分で自分のプレゼンテーションを評価する自己評価 (Self-Evaluation) と、クラスメイトのプレゼンテーションを評価し、改善点を指摘するピア・レヴュー (Peer Review/Evaluation) があります。

自己評価（Self-Evaluation）

自己評価では、まず、自分たちの作ったプレゼンテーションの原稿を以下のチェックリストを使って確認します。もし、No になったら、前の Unit に戻って改善しましょう。これを行った後は、想定される質問を考え、リハーサルです。

Exercise A

次の（　）内に下の選択肢から適当な文を選び記入しましょう。

Checklist for Presentation Structure

Introduction		
Did I/we offer a proper greeting to the audience?		Yes / No
(a.)		Yes / No
Did I/we explain the structure of our talk?		Yes / No
Body		
Did I/we state our points clearly?		Yes / No
(b.)		Yes / No
Did I/we provide convincing evidence for the points?		Yes / No
Did I/we make references to the sources of information?		Yes / No
Conclusion		
(c.)		Yes / No
Did I/we thank the audience and invite them to ask questions?		Yes / No

［選択肢］

1. Did I/we use effective signal words/ transitions like "for example?"
2. Did I/we summarize the key point(s)?
3. Did I/we tell the main idea of our talk?

■ リストが完成したら、自分（たち）のプレゼンテーションの原稿を再確認してみましょう。

　原稿が完成したら、もう一度読み直してみましょう。プレゼンテーションの最後には、オーディエンスから質問を受け付けることも大切なプレゼンテーションの一部です。想定される質問を以下に考えてみましょう。

Exercise B

予想される質問とその答えを 2 つ以上考えてみましょう。答えは英語にしましょう。

[Questions]

1. ....

2. ....

3. ....

[Answers]

1. ....

2. ....

3. ....

Exercise C

次の各文がどんな種類の質問にふさわしい返答か考えて、線で結んでみましょう。

1. To be honest, I think that raises a different issue.　　　A. good questions

2. That's a very good question.　　　B. difficult questions

3. Interesting! What do you think?　　　C. unnecessary questions

4. Well, as I mentioned earlier,...　　　D. irrelevant questions

いよいよリハーサルです。リハーサルを行うのは、英語の発音やことば使いのチェックだけでなく、プレゼンテーションの内容をしっかり飲み込んでいるかどうかを確かめるためです。特に、英文が自分でも覚えられないくらい長く複雑になっていませんか。発表者（presenter）にとって分かりにくい英語が聴衆（audience）に分かることはありませんね。

Exercise D

次の Evaluation Sheet は、自分のプレゼンテーションのリハーサルでも使い、また、他のクラスメイトのプレゼンテーションを評価する時にも使うものです。評価項目と内容の意味を確かめながら、適当な語を下の選択肢から入れてみましょう。

Evaluation Sheet

Category	Item	Evaluation			
聴衆への配慮 Audience Focus	(a.　　　　　　　　　　　)	1 poor　2 fair 3 good　4 excellent			
	Interaction (Q & A)	1	2	3	4
内容 Contents	Structure and organization	1	2	3	4
	Clear and logical examples	1	2	3	4
身振り・話しぶり Delivery	Good voice and articulation / Smooth delivery	1	2	3	4
	Posture / (b.　　　　　　)	1	2	3	4
表現・ことば使い Language	Transitions / (c.　　　　　)	1	2	3	4
	(d.　　　　　　　)	1	2	3	4
資料 Materials	Contribution to understanding	1	2	3	4
	Slides	1	2	3	4
説得力 Persuasiveness	(e.　　　　　　　)	1	2	3	4
	Benefits for audience	1	2	3	4

1. Evidence　　　　2. Expression　　　　3. Eye contact
4. Signal words　　5. Timing and punctuality

ピア・レヴュー（Peer Review/Evaluation ）

　Exercise D で完成させた Evaluation Sheet を参考にクラスメイトのプレゼンテーションを評価してみましょう。評価に使う下の図表は、レーダー・チャート (radar chart) といい、数値をイメージ化し、全体のバランスが分かるものです。クラスメイトのプレゼンテーションを評価することは、自分のプレゼンテーションの改善にもつながります。Evaluation Sheet に比べて評価の刻み（目盛り）を増やしました。

Presentation No.: ....

Presenter(s): ....

Theme/Title: ....

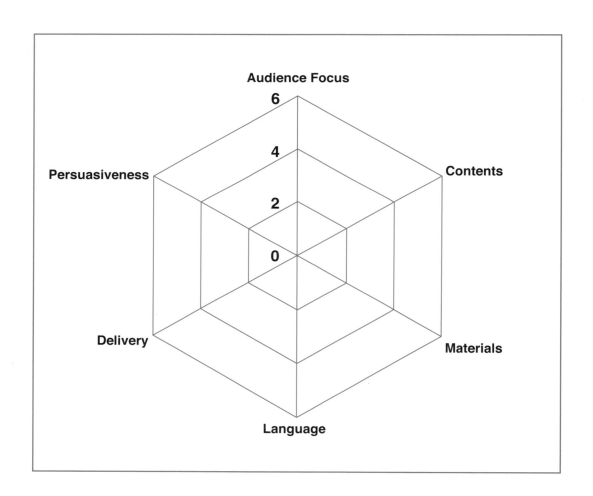

Notes

Appendix

モデルプレゼンテーション原稿

①〜⑩の番号は右ページのスライドが表示されるところです。

① Good morning, everyone. I'm happy to have an opportunity to speak to you today. ② My presentation today is about a health issue which is a concern for many university students. The purpose of this presentation is to offer some ideas regarding the problem of lack of sleep for those who begin to live alone. ③ In my brief presentation I will outline three possible solutions to tackle this problem. So, let's move on to how you can maintain a healthy sleeping pattern.

④ First of all, in order to sleep well, you should get regular exercise. Jogging, swimming or just taking a walk has a very positive effect on our overall physical health. ⑤ According to numerous academic studies, moderate exercise on a daily basis contributes to the quality of sleep. ⑥ Another way to improve your sleep pattern is to make sure that you go to bed at a regular hour. ⑦ According to medical reports, if you go to bed around the same time every night, you will fall asleep more easily. Even if you have a lot of assignments, try getting up a bit earlier instead of staying up late. ⑧ Finally, make sure that your bedroom is not too hot. ⑨ Many scientific reports suggest that we fall asleep faster in a cool room and enjoy a more restful sleep. This is especially important in the hot summer months.

⑩ In conclusion, good sleep is necessary in order to have a productive and healthy life. Today I described three steps you can take to improve the quality of your sleep: exercise, go to bed at a regular hour and keep your room cool at night. ⑪ That concludes my speech and I will take any questions you may have. ⑫

①

②

③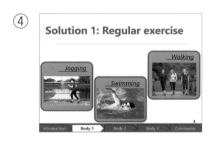

④

⑤

⑥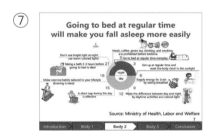

⑦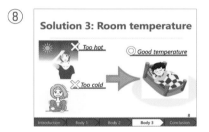

⑧

⑨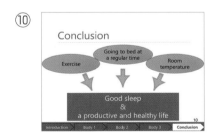

⑩

⑪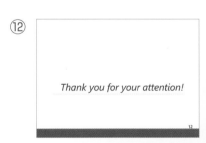

⑫ *Thank you for your attention!*

Notes

Message Delivered <Lower Intermediate> [B-901]

パターンで学ぶパラグラフ・ライティングとプレゼンテーション入門〈基礎編〉

1 刷	2020年3月26日
3 刷	2023年8月30日

著 者	レオニード・ヨッフェ	Leonid Yoffe
	千葉　敦	Atsushi Chiba
	青田　庄真	Shoma Aota
	森田　彰	Akira Morita

発行者　南雲一範　Kazunori Nagumo
発行所　株式会社　南雲堂
〒162-0801　東京都新宿区山吹町361
NAN'UN-DO Publishing Co., Ltd.
361 Yamabuki-cho, Shinjuku-ku, Tokyo 162-0801, Japan
振替口座: 00160-0-46863
TEL:　03-3268-2311（営業部：学校関係）
　　　03-3268-2384（営業部：書店関係）
　　　03-3268-2387（編集部）
FAX:　03-3269-2486

編集者	加藤　敦
装　丁	銀月堂
組　版	Office haru
検　印	省　略
コード	ISBN978-4-523-17901-6　C0082

Printed in Japan

E-mail　nanundo@post.email.ne.jp
URL　https://www.nanun-do.co.jp/